A FIRST HISTORY OF
CORNWALL

A FIRST
HISTORY OF
CORNWALL

JOHN JENKIN

DYLLANSOW TRURAN

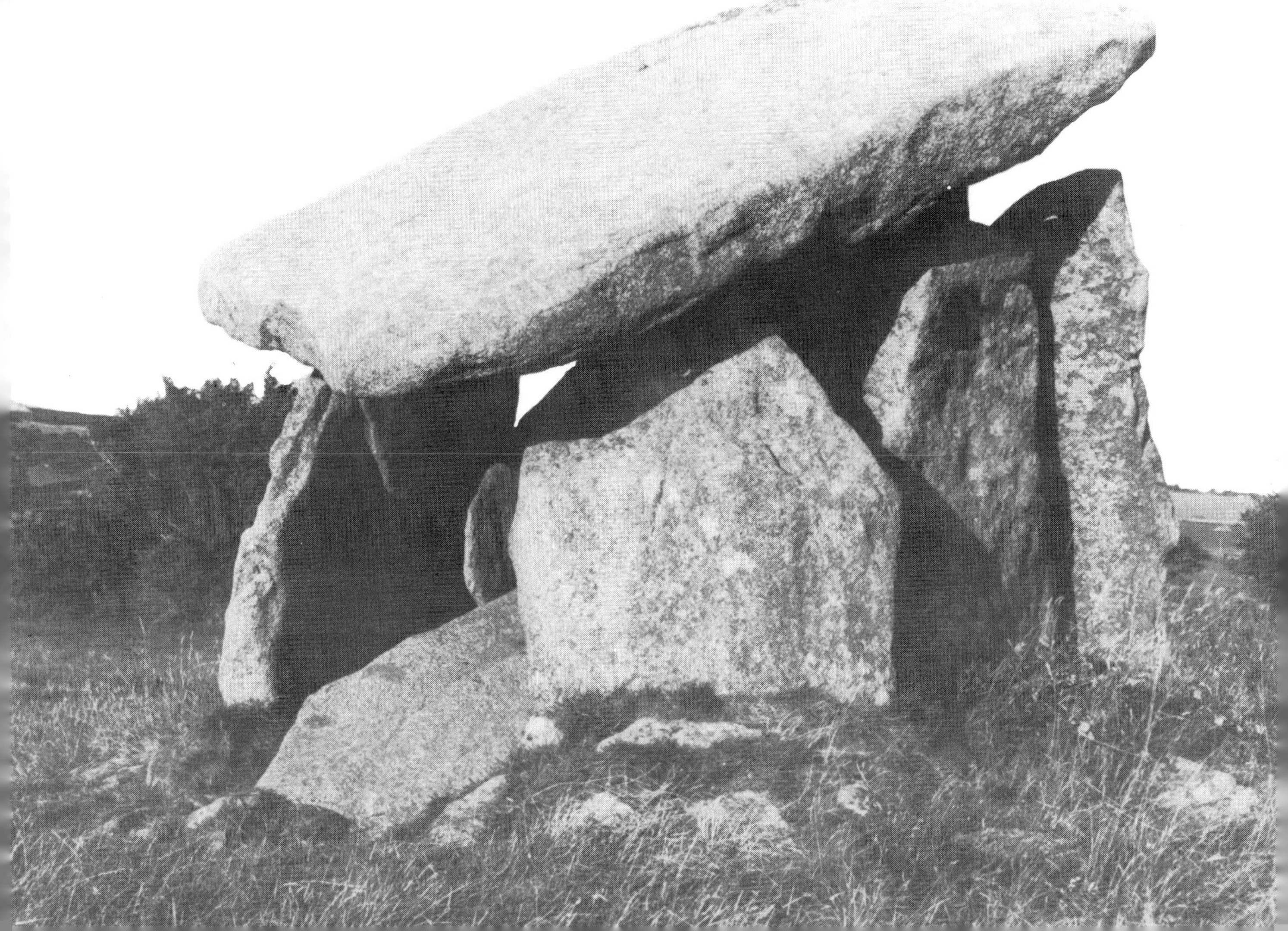

Dyllansow Truran
Cornish Publications
Trewolsta, Trewirgie, Redruth, Cornwall

Drawings by Craig Weatherhill
Photograph of St Michael's Mount by Geoff Hichens,
Gulval, Penzance

First published 1984
Reprinted 1987

Printed and bound in Great Britain by
A. Wheaton & Co. Ltd, Exeter

ISBN 0 907566 85 5 Non Net
ISBN 0 907566 74 X Net

CONTENTS

INTRODUCTION

This is a book about Cornwall and the people who have lived here for more than eight thousand years. It is about men and women who were famous and many who were just ordinary folk whose names have never been recorded. It is a book about how people lived, about brave deeds, about clever inventions and how Cornwall has become what it is today, a part of the British Isles but so very different from the other counties.

Cornwall is almost an island. The River Tamar, which forms its eastern border, almost cuts it off from the rest of Britain and the sea is its border on the north, west and south. Because of this and because it is a Celtic land, it has a character all its own. The countryside is different, the older houses and villages are different, the place-names are not English and the real Cornish people do not consider themselves as English, any more than the Welsh, Scots or Irish consider themselves as English. This is not a romantic or fanciful notion. It is a matter of history, culture and race.

By reading this book you are showing that you are interested in knowing more about Cornwall. It is natural to be interested in the history of the place in which we live. We all show that interest at an early age when we ask our parents and grand-parents for stories about their young lives and what life was like 'in the olden days'. What we are today and the way we live now are the results of the struggles and achievements of all those who have lived before us. We, in our turn, are making the history of tomorrow.

How do we know about the past? First, we are told about it by those who are still alive. This is perhaps the most fascinating way of all, listening to those who were actually present when exciting things happened. Second, we can look at films and photographs, a way which goes back about a hundred years. This is a long time for us but not long in history, when we remember that man has been around for at least a hundred-thousand years. Third, we can read about the past in books and documents. In our country these go back about fifteen-hundred years.

For information about life before this, we have to rely on the story told by the objects left behind, tools and weapons, ornaments and toys, the remains of houses and household articles. Here history becomes a detective story and we have to rely on the skill and knowledge of experts. It is a study which is never completed because new discoveries are always being made.

Whether you are truly Cornish with a family which has been living in Cornwall longer than anyone can remember or trace, whether you are Cornish by birth, whether part of your family is Cornish, or whether you have come to Cornwall to live, you will find something of interest here. If it helps you to see Cornwall with new eyes and with a greater understanding of its unique history, this book will have served a useful purpose. Perhaps one day you will add your own famous contribution to the land of Kernow, the Celtic name for Cornwall.

Title page: **Trethevy Quoit near St. Cleer. The remaining burial chamber of a Bronze Age barrow.**

Left: **Cornwall's badge on the Tamar Bridge, with a fisherman, miner, chough, fifteen bezants and the motto 'One and All'.**

BC

OLD AND MIDDLE STONE AGES

Hunters

Not many people
in Cornwall at
this time

4500

THE NEW STONE AGE

The first farmers came

The first villages

The first pottery

Tools of stone and flint

2500

THE BRONZE AGE

New people came

They were metal workers
as well as farmers

Built stone circles, menhirs
and barrows of different kinds

Villages on high ground

Bronze tools, weapons and
ornaments

800

THE IRON AGE

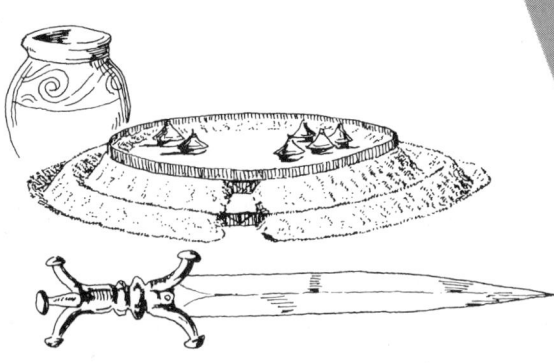

The first Celts
came to Cornwall

Hill forts and
cliff forts

Tools and weapons
of iron

IBC

The birth of Jesus

I AD

Chapter 1

CORNWALL'S EARLIEST PEOPLE

We do not know when the first people lived in Cornwall but it was certainly a very long time ago. Many thousands of years before the birth of Jesus there were primitive families living in the island of Britain, wandering from place to place in small groups in an everlasting search for food. They were a hairy race, rather ape-like in appearance, and their simple tools and weapons were of stone and bone. Their personal possessions were few and their homes were caves or crudely-built shelters.

Few traces of these Early Stone Age people have been found in Cornwall and it is probable that not many of them lived here at that period. It may even be that the items found were brought here by later visitors and that in these early times, Cornwall was an empty land; its high, bare, windswept moors, tree-covered lower slopes and valleys, and gale-lashed cliffs and beaches, known only to the birds and roaming animals.

Around 8000 B.C., a new race came to Britain from across the swampy land and shallow waters which then separated us from Europe. They too were simple in their ways and lived wherever they could find food. Some of them came to Cornwall and their remains have been found, especially near the coasts, where they found the best materials for tools and weapons. This period is known as the Middle Stone Age. The men hunted and fished, the women and children collected roots and berries, clothing was made from skins and food was roasted over open fires, for as yet nobody had discovered how to make pots. By our standards, they were primitive but also very skilled at making the best use of the materials around them.

Coming nearer to our own time but still long ago, about 4500 B.C., new settlers came from the lands on the northern side of the Mediterranean. They brought improved tools, which helped them to clear the bushes and smaller trees, a knowledge of farming and the art of making pottery. They lived a more settled life and built small villages with houses of stone and thatch. Their best known living site in Cornwall is on the top of Carn Brea hill at Redruth, where a large number of arrowheads and some pottery have been excavated.

As the centuries passed, other groups of settlers came to Cornwall, bringing with them new skills. The most important of these was the knowledge of metal-working with copper and tin. The discovery that these two metals could be combined to make bronze was an enormous step forward in Man's development. The fact that both these ores were to be found in Cornwall made it both well-known and prosperous.

The era known as the Bronze Age began, in Cornwall, about 2500 B.C. It did not, of course, start in one particular year or on one special day but was a gradual process over several centuries. We know that merchants came here from distant lands in search of tin and copper and that a flourishing trade grew up, not only in the raw materials but in finished goods that were exchanged for articles brought in by the visiting traders. Many fine bronze tools, weapons and ornaments have been found along the lines of the old trading routes where there were good landing-places and well-beaten tracks between the most prosperous villages. Ornaments of gold have also been discovered. These were probably brought from Ireland, where gold was available in some quantity at that time. In 1865, two beautiful gold collars were found at Harlyn Bay and others have been found near Hayle and Tintagel. These are all on the north coast, on the direct sea route between Ireland and south-west Britain.

Many of the early Bronze Age villages have disappeared. Others have had later settlements built on the same sites so that the Bronze Age remains have been lost, buried deep or mixed with debris from following centuries. There are, however, plenty of village remains still to be seen, particularly on Bodmin Moor and the uplands of West Penwith. Excavations have shown that the small houses were circular, with low stone walls and roofs of thatch and branches. Traces of farming have also been found so our early ancestors were really quite well-organized, living in villages with 'factories' for metalworking, cultivating the land and keeping animals, and carrying on a busy trade with people across the seas.

Tools in use before the Bronze Age

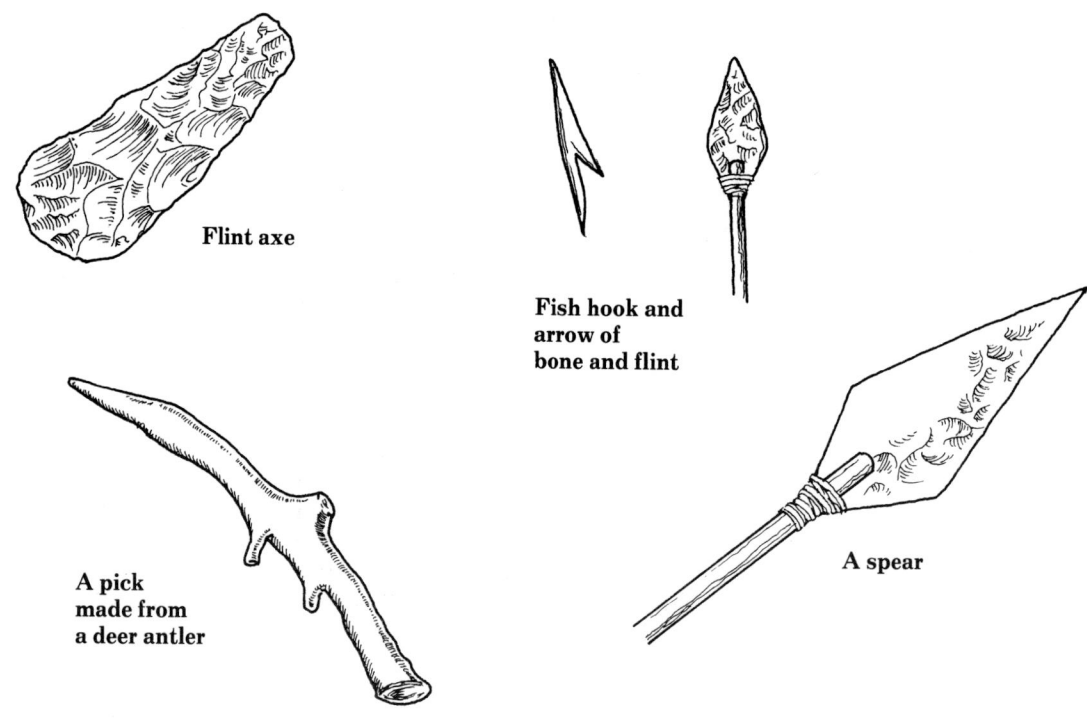

Flint axe

Fish hook and
arrow of
bone and flint

A pick
made from
a deer antler

A spear

Bronze Age tools and weapons

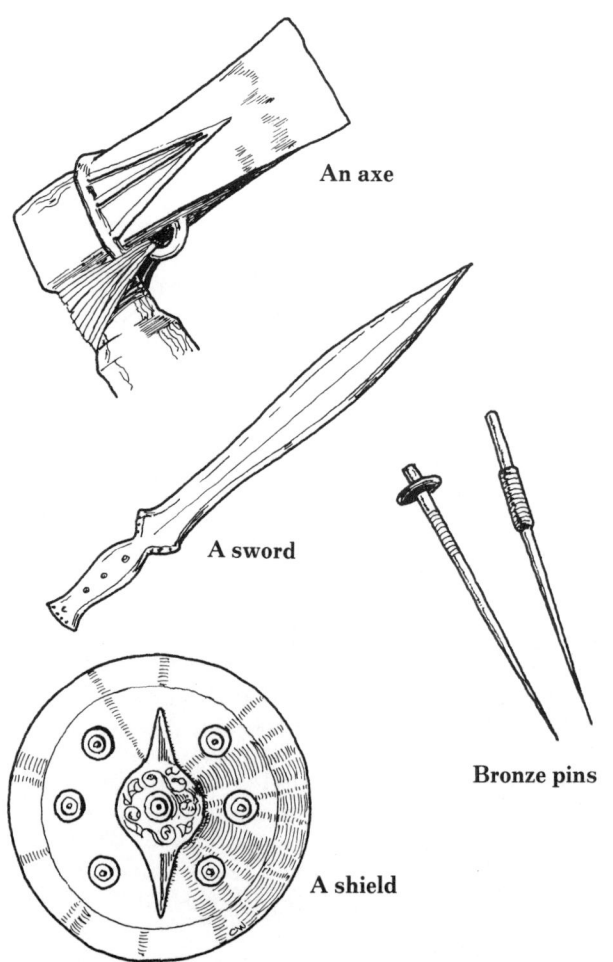

An axe

A sword

Bronze pins

A shield

Bronze Age farming was very simple. There were no fields as we know them. The gentler hill slopes were cleared in long narrow strips and, when the land was exhausted, cultivation was moved to a new piece of ground. Ploughing was done across the slope so the earth tended to move downhill every year, forming ridges along the sides of the hills. These can still be seen in some places, although it takes an expert eye to distinguish them from the natural bumps and hollows.

Cattle were very small in size, as were all the animals kept by the early farmers. They were about the size of the Dexter breed kept on a few modern farms, and sometimes seen at agricultural shows. Nearly all their animals were killed at the beginning of winter as it was not possible to feed them once the summer grass stopped growing. Winter was a hard time for man and beast alike.

Much Bronze Age pottery has been found. It was made for everyday use in cooking and storage so it is rather thick and the decorations simple. Sometimes, the potter made patterns with a pointed stick or by pressing a piece of cord into the soft clay before firing it.

A great deal of pottery has been discovered in the graves of the period and the Bronze Age has been called 'The Age of the Dead' because much of our knowledge about it has come from burial sites.

About four thousand years ago, when the Late Stone Age in Britain was merging with the early Bronze Age, there was a custom of burying the important and respected dead in stone tombs. The idea had perhaps been brought by settlers from the lands around the Mediterranean, in imitation of the great pyramids of Egypt, the tombs of the Pharaohs. The stone tombs in Britain are not nearly as large or spectacular as those, however. Many have been completely destroyed while others have been partly demolished, by man or by weathering.

In Cornwall, we know nothing about the actual people for whom the tombs were made. Since even the smallest tomb required great labour to build, the occupants must have been important to the Bronze Age tribes. In Britain, the great period of tomb building lasted about five hundred years, from 2500 B.C., to 2000 B.C. Archaeologists call it the Megalithic Period, the name coming from two Greek words, 'megas' = great and 'lithos' = stone.

There are the remains of many of them in Cornwall, especially in the west and in the Isles of Scilly. We call them cromlechs or quoits, both names refer to megalithic tomb chambers. All that now remains of most of them is the large stone box which once housed the dead body, or the ashes when the body had been cremated. They were built by raising a number of huge granite slabs into an upright box shape and roofing them with a single slab called a capstone. The number of upright stones varies but is generally three to five. Sometimes, the capstone is horizontal. Sometimes, it slopes at a sharp angle.

The box or chamber having been formed, the remains were placed within it in an urn or cist (a stone 'chest'). An enormous mound of earth was then built over the whole, sealing it and forming a monument visible from a distance. Archaeologists call them chamber tombs. Sometimes, a stone passage was built from the outside of the mound to the inner chamber so that the tomb could be used for more than one burial. These are known as entrance graves.

Over the centuries, wind and rain have washed away the earth surrounding the chambers. Farmers often took away the soil to spread it over their land leaving the stone cromlechs standing as they were originally erected. Treasure-seekers have damaged them, removing their contents and, in several instances, the stones have fallen or have been pulled down. Much valuable information has thus been lost.

There are three good examples of cromlechs left for us to visit. On a hillside outside St Cleer, near Liskeard, is Trethevy Quoit. It is small but un-damaged except for the removal of the earth mound and is certainly worth seeking. Chun cromlech, near the Land's End, is also at the top of a barren hillside and probably gives a better feeling of the distant past than any other. From the site, one can see the rolling moors and the sea and, standing there with the wind rustling the grass and only the birds for company, the visitor can easily imagine the reverence of the ancient people for the spot and the chieftain for whom they built the tomb. Not many miles away, by the roadside at Lanyon Farm, stands Lanyon Quoit. This was once a large chamber. The capstone was replaced some years ago and some stones are now missing so, although impressive in size, it is not an original example.

Chun Cromlech, Zennor. Nearby are the remains of Chun Castle, an Iron Age hill fort.

Also on the moors of West Penwith is a curious stone called the Men an Tol, the 'holed stone'. Standing upright amid a number of fallen slabs, it has a hole in it large enough to crawl through. Many years ago, local folk believed that it had magical powers and that crawling through it would cure rheumatism and other diseases of the bones. In fact, it was probably part of a chamber tomb which had two compartments, the holed stone being the link between the two parts.

Cromlechs are usually found on the high moors because that is where the ancient people lived and because the tombs were a visible reminder to the living of the glories of the dead.

Tombs are not the only man-made works of the Megalithic Period. There are twenty-one stone circles in Cornwall, and scores of single standing stones or menhirs.

Stone circles are thought to have been important meeting-places. They were formed by placing large upright stones, often weighing many tons each, in a circle large enough to hold several hundred people. The number of stones used varies but nineteen is a common number wherever these circles are found. Sometimes, a single large stone is to be found in the centre or nearby. Many of the stones have fallen or have been taken away to make hedges or gateposts.

Whatever their purpose, they were very carefully laid out and seem to have had some connection with the movements of the sun and the stars, which suggests that ancient man had a considerable knowledge of astronomy and may have used them for religious purposes. Like cromlechs, they are found in places other than Cornwall and there are references to similar structures in the Old Testament of the Bible.

The Men an Tol. A holed stone on the moors between Penzance and Land's End.
It is probably the remains of a burial chamber, although legend said that if children suffering from rickets (a bone disease) were passed through the hole,
they would be cured.

The Merry Maidens, a circle of nineteen stones near Penzance.

We read that when the Israelites crossed the Jordan they took twelve stones from the river, one for each of the twelve tribes, and that Joshua erected them in Gilgal, which is the Hebrew word for a circle or wheel. Also, in the Book of Samuel, we read that Samuel 'judged Israel all the days of his life. And he went from year to year in circuit to Bethel and Gilgal and Mizpah, and judged Israel in all these places.'

It does seem likely, therefore, that they were places for some kind of worship or counsel. Each one may have been for the use of the tribes who lived nearby, or they may have been part of a much larger organization about which we know nothing at the moment.

Perhaps one day we shall discover their purpose but at the moment we can only guess. There are many legends concerning them. Our ancestors supposed that each stone was a human being who had been turned from flesh to stone because of some wickedness, just as Lot's wife had been turned into a pillar of salt in the Bible story in the Book of Genesis.

Near Penzance is a circle known as The Merry Maidens and nearby are two single upright stones called The Pipers. Legend says that the nineteen stones were once nineteen young girls who danced wickedly on a Sunday and that the two stones were the pipers who played music for them. On Bodmin Moor, near the village of Minions, are the remains of three circles placed together. If they were meeting-places, this one must have been of special importance. It is known as The Hurlers, because legend says that the people played the game of Hurling the Ball on Sunday and were turned to stone because of it. The Merry Maidens also has a Cornish name, Dawns Men, from 'dons' meaning dancing and 'men' meaning stone. You can find the Nine Stones or Nine Maidens near Land's End and another circle by the same name at Wendron, near Redruth. On Bodmin Moor there are also the Trippet Stones and the Stripple Stones. The maps show them as *Stone Circle* or by the legendary name.

The Hurlers on Bodmin Moor.
The remains of three circles placed together.

If little is known about the purpose of the stone circles, even less is understood about the single stones, or menhirs. The name is Cornish, from 'men'=stone and 'hyr'=long. Thus, menhir=long stone. Traces of burials have been found beneath some of them so perhaps they mark the grave of somebody important, or the site of an important event.

Times and customs change and as the Bronze Age progressed so the burial customs of the people altered. The practice of building stone chambered tombs died out but the bodies or ashes were still buried beneath huge earth mounds known as barrows. They are marked on maps as *Tumulus,* or *Tumuli* if there is more than one. If you examine a good map of Cornwall and look at the moorland areas of the east and west you will find scores of them.

There are several different types of barrow to be found in Britain. Some are long mounds, some are circular and some have ditches dug around them as well. All, save one, of the barrows in Cornwall are circular. Like those containing chambered tombs, nearly all barrows have been excavated, usually by people who knew nothing about archaeology and who destroyed much valuable information. A number of objects have been preserved, however, and may be seen in good museums such the R.I.C. Museum in Truro. In fact, most of what we know about the Bronze Age in Cornwall comes from the objects which have been found in barrow graves: bronze axes, daggers, cups and bowls, ornaments and beads.

By the end of the Bronze Age, about 1000 B.C. to 600 B.C., barrow building was dying out and when the Iron Age peoples came the custom ceased altogether, the dead being buried in cemeteries.

We have seen how Cornwall was gradually populated by settlers from the Mediterranean lands and from the area we now call Spain. Each new race brought with it new skills and different customs. Tools and weapons improved, from simple stone implements to bronze. Pottery came and was improved, the increasing skill of the potter seen in the shapes of the pots made and the decorations used on them. Man changed from a wandering hunter and fisherman to being a settled farmer and manufacturer.

All this took an incredibly long time, about 15 000 years. That is seven times longer than the period of time which has passed since the birth of Christ. We know how great have been the changes since then and how many things have been discovered. It is, perhaps, hard for us to imagine the enormous length of time before that event.

Between about 1000 B.C. and 500 B.C., a new people came to Britain from across the Channel. They brought with them a knowledge of the production and use of iron and in time of peace they, like the late Bronze Age people, were farmers and traders. The existing inhabitants of Britain did not welcome them and their settlement was accompanied by a good deal of fighting.

Gradually, but surely, they established themselves in southern Britain and from there they spread to become the principal race in these islands. Their arrival in Cornwall has been put at about 800 B.C.

It is these people, called Celts by the Romans, who are the real ancestors of the Cornish, the Welsh and the Bretons. Their language, their love of song and story and their fierce independence have survived to this day, and their descendants survived in the west long after the coming of the English races.

Our knowledge of them comes from their living sites and their forts, for their cemeteries are unmarked, unlike the burial places of the Bronze Age. They lived in villages, with small houses of stone and thatch, with barns and storehouses and protective walls of stakes. Around them lay their fields, in long narrow strips, with enclosures for their animals. They worked in tin, bronze and iron, making implements not only for their own use but also for export. Very few iron tools have been found because iron rusts quickly but an enormous quantity of Iron Age pottery and domestic articles has been unearthed.

In West Cornwall, houses were sometimes arranged in small groups around a central courtyard, with stone paths connecting them. The best example is at Chysauster, not far from Penzance. Of course, the roofs and their timbers have long since disappeared, but the low walls remain and the fireplaces and grinding stones are still there for all to see.

In many villages there are traces of tin smelting and we know from ancient writings, and the discovery of pottery from the Mediterranean, that there was a flourishing trade with overseas merchants. One ancient writer tells us that the people of the south-west were called the Dumnonii and their land Dumnonia.

Iron Age villages are numerous in the country, far too numerous to be mentioned by name. You will find them in abundance on the map, marked as *Hut Circles* or *Ancient Village.* Many of them are on the same sites as earlier Bronze Age villages. Carn Brea is an example, and the scores of hut remains on the slopes of Roughtor on Bodmin Moor show that it was inhabited for centuries by these early peoples.

Because they were invaders, the Celts had to defend themselves against attacks by the earlier inhabitants and it was their custom to fortify the tops of hills near their villages by digging deep ditches around the summits and further defending the enclosures thus made by palisades of sharp stakes. It was not usual to live in them. They were refuges in time of trouble. In Cornwall there are many hill forts and promontory forts, built on cliffs where the headlands could be easily defended by a ditch across the landward side and the steep cliffs on the other sides. Like the villages, they are numerous and are shown on maps by the name of *Castle* or *Camp.* Cornish words are sometimes used in their names. Hence we get place-names containing the word Car, Gear or Caer, from 'ker'=fort; or variations of the word 'dinas'=hill fort. Some examples are, <u>Car</u>dinham, <u>Caer</u>hays, <u>Car</u>bis Bay, Tre<u>gear</u>; Castle-an-<u>dinas</u>, Pen<u>dinas</u>.

To attack one of these forts was a daunting task. The attackers had to cross open ground or climb the sides of a steep hill, negotiate fences of sharp stakes and deep ditches, all in the face of a hail of stones and spears. Most forts had more than one set of ditches and ramparts, with entrance gates especially well-defended and placed to make successful assaults almost impossible. Even the Romans, in their later conquest, with a large and well-trained army, found the capture of these forts very expensive in lives.

Four views of the Iron Age fort by the Cheesewring. Thousands of granite boulders were piled up by the Celts to make this defence. From this hill-top a sentry could see enemies advancing from miles away.

By the time of Christ, Britain and its Celtic inhabitants were well known throughout western Europe and the Mediterranean. It was known that they had a settled life, were skilled in farming and metalworking and that they were flourishing traders.

It was known that the land of the Dumnonii, as all the south-west was then called, was a valuable source of that precious metal, tin. It was also known that the Celts were very fierce fighters and would resist strongly any attempt at invasion and conquest.

In Rome, successive Emperors collected all the information they could about Britain and resolved to add it to the Roman Empire as soon as possible. It was too valuable to remain outside Roman control.

In 55 B.C., the Roman general Caius Julius Caesar landed in southern Britain with a small force to spy out the land and to assess the problems of an invasion. Nearly one hundred years later, in A.D. 43, the Emperor Claudius decided that the time had come and a large army landed to begin the war which resulted in the Roman Conquest and a period of Roman rule which lasted four hundred years.

Roman influence on the Dumnonii was small compared with the effect on southern, eastern and central Britain and the people kept most of their Celtic ways. The English invaders who followed the Romans brought a whole new way of life and a new language. In the centuries from A.D. 400, to about A.D. 900, Celtic life and language was forced ever westward until it existed only in Wales and the land beyond the Tamar. It was the English invasion which created Cornwall and made Cornwall different from England in so many ways.

Some Things To Do

1 Look in other history books to see how the people of the Stone Age, the Bronze Age and the Iron Age lived. Draw some pictures of their houses and the things they used.

2 Visit your local museum and look for tools, weapons and pottery from this period.

3 Look at the Ordnance Survey maps of Cornwall, especially that for the area in which you live. Look for the words:

    Tumulus or Tumuli   Settlement
    Hut Circles   Stone Circles
    Cromlech   Quoit
    Castle   Earthwork

Visit some of them.

4 Make model huts and villages or a hill fort.

Chapter 2

CORNWALL IN ROMAN TIMES and THE COMING OF THE ENGLISH

The Roman conquest of Britain took many years. In A.D. 60, seventeen years after the first landing, the Roman soldiers were just beginning their conquest of the lowland areas of Wales and it was thirty-five years before they had effective control there. The mountain regions of central Britain and the north remained mainly Celtic. The great wall built by the Emperor Hadrian to keep out the northern tribes was not built until A.D. 123, when he decided that the wild lands of the north were of no value to the Empire.

In the first century of Roman occupation, there were a number of serious rebellions by the most patriotic Celts in southern and eastern Britain but, eventually, Roman rule was firmly established in the area now covered by England and Wales. Those Celts in what is now the heartland of England came under the total influence of Roman ways, Roman customs, Roman dress and Roman language. In fact, many Celts took pride in being Roman citizens and grew to despise their country-men who clung to the old Celtic ways.

The lands of the Dumnonii, now called Devon and Cornwall, were not very important to Rome and were far enough away from the mainstream of life to be no threat to Roman rule. A Roman city was established at Exeter and from there the region was easily controlled.

To the west of Exeter, and especially beyond the Tamar, was a wild, trackless land, thinly populated and without large towns. The Tamar was a great barrier and just beyond it was a huge barren and swampy moor which made access even more difficult. Along the coast were high cliffs and few safe landing-places, except in the south.

The Celts of Cornwall were, therefore, not greatly disturbed by the Roman occupation. Their valuable tin trade continued, Roman officials and soldiers visited, some Roman ways were adopted by those few people in regular touch with the new rulers but, generally, life went on unchanged.

For these reasons, Roman remains are few in Cornwall. Some Roman milestones have been found on the old tin trading routes to the coast, and traces of about twenty small forts. The only one which seems to have been occupied for any length of time is at Tregear, near Bodmin. This is thought to have been used continuously for about twenty-five years.

A great quantity of Roman money has been found, mainly near the coast where the tin trade flourished. Some of the hoards have contained hundreds of coins and we wonder what caused them to be hidden or abandoned. 160 were found at Breage and 2500 at Caerhays. In 1967, a farmer ploughing his land found more than 1000, so it is likely that there are many thousands more waiting to be discovered. Money indicates that there was trade and the presence of so much money means that the trade was a valuable one.

When people become prosperous they usually build large houses to live in and we know that in England many rich Romans or romanized Celts built fine villas in the Roman style for themselves and their families. Only one such villa has so far been found in Cornwall, at Magor Farm, near Camborne, in 1931. Tiles and decorated plaster work were found, along with coins and other objects but it does not seem to have been a particularly grand house.

Some experts now think that there are more Roman remains in Cornwall than we realize and that when more excavations have been carried out, many interesting things will be found to add to our store of knowledge.

About the year A.D. 400, the city state of Rome was increasingly beset by enemies and the great Roman Empire began to crumble. The legions were called home and, as trade slackened and the daily government of the provinces became more difficult and less important, the officials and their families went too. Within a short time, all the Romans had left, leaving their subject Celts without law and order or strong government.

As they hoped to return one day, they left the country in charge of Britons who had been trained in their ways but, whenever a strong leader goes, squabbles break out among the subjects left behind and there is usually a time of decay and trouble. The peaceful Britain organized so well by the Romans fell into decline, leaving the land open to troubles within and invasion from without. The eastern shores had long been troubled by bands of raiders from across the North Sea. They had been kept at bay by Roman ships, forts and soldiers but now that these strong defenders had departed, who was there to keep them out?

With the departure of the Roman legions, the raids by the Angles, Jutes, Saxons and Danes increased in number and strength. Within a short time, the invaders came to settle with their families and their belongings. History tells us that two of the first great leaders were brothers, Hengist and Horsa, and that Hengist took a small kingdom for himself called Kent, which the Romans had called Cantium, probably from a Celtic word. The name England now appeared, coming from the tribe of the Angles, who called the new country Angle-land, which later became England.

In time, the Saxons became the most important tribes and other small kingdoms were set up. They were known as the lands of the East Saxons, the Middle Saxons, the South Saxons and the West Saxons. The first three names are still the names of three English counties, Essex, Middlesex and Sussex, while the name of Wessex is still used to describe Dorset and part of southern England.

The first invaders were not Christian but worshipped many gods and they were unable to read or write. They had no use for the fine things left by the Romans so they were destroyed or allowed to fall into ruin. Christianity and learning almost disappeared from their land although there were still Christian Kingdoms in the northern part of what is now England, such as Cumbria and Elmet. For four or five hundred years after the end of Roman rule, the country suffered from wars and destructions while the invaders battled between themselves and the native Celts for mastery of the land. This time is known as the Dark Ages because of the troubles and because there are very few pieces of writing which survive to tell us exactly what went on.

The Celts in the west, those who had been least affected by Roman rule, fought most fiercely against the Saxons and it was four hundred years before they were finally conquered. By the year A.D. 700, the West Saxons had reached the Bristol Channel and the Celts of Wales were cut off from the Celts of the south-west. Many battles took place in west Devon and north and east Cornwall. The Saxon King Egbert made a conquest in A.D. 814, but ten years later he had to come again to make the Celts submit.

The last great battle took place on Hingston Down near Callington, in A.D. 838. The West Welsh, as the Saxons called the Celts of the south-west, to distinguish them from the Celts of Wales, joined forces with an army of Danes and met the Saxons on the barren moor. The result was a great victory for the Saxons and the western Celts never really recovered. One hundred years later, the Saxon King Athelstan conquered the far west and from this time onward the English rule was complete.

The Men Scryfa (the inscribed stone.)
This stone is believed to date from the fifth or sixth century, and is inscribed in Latin.

Legend tells us about a number of Celtic kings at this time. We do not know much about them except their names, Rialobran, Gereint, Mark, Doniert and Arthur. The last is such a vague figure that we do not know if he really had any connection with Cornwall at all. His legend is mentioned later in Chapter Eight.

The names of the other heroes appear carved on large stones, found throughout Cornwall. Most of the inscriptions are in Latin. On the moors of west Cornwall there is a large stone called, in Cornish, the Men Scryfa, meaning 'the inscribed or written stone'. It simply reads, *Rialobrani Cunovali fili,* or Rialobran son of Cunoval. Rialobrani has been interpreted as meaning 'Royal Raven'. Near Fowey is a stone which bears a latin inscription which reads, in English, 'Here lies Drustanus, son of Cunomorus' and these names are thought to refer to King Mark and his son Tristan. By the road from Minions to Liskeard in East Cornwall is King Doniert's Stone. Doniert was drowned in a nearby river in A.D. 878, and is believed to have been a Cornish king called Dumgarth. These men were among the last of the independent Celtic chieftains of the west.

Two views of King Doniert's Stone. This broken memorial was set up to the Cornish King who was drowned in the river Dreyne about 1100 years ago. It is inscribed in Latin DONIERT ROGAVIT PRO ANIMA, which means 'Doniert ordered (this to be set up) for (the good of) his soul'.

So, we have come to an important point in Cornwall's story. Much of the old land of Britain has been conquered by the Saxons and is now called England. The last true Celts, in Cornwall and Wales, are cut off from each other and henceforth their common language develops along different lines. The Cornish Celts are under the domination of the Saxons and from this time their history is bound up with that of the English.

Although the name Cornwall has been used in this story to describe the land west of the Tamar, it must be remembered that it was not so called until the coming of the English. The far west was the land of the Dumnonii or Cornovii, the 'hill-dwellers'. Later the Saxons referred to all the western Celts as Wealas, meaning 'strangers'. From this word Wealas came the name of Wales. Cornwall came from a combination of Cornovii and Wealas, meaning 'the Welsh of the West' or the 'Hill-dwellers' of the West.

We will now call our people Cornish and their land, Cornwall. For several hundred years more, they kept their old Celtic language. Indeed, in the far west, English influence remained small for a very long time after the English language and English ways became dominant in the east of our land.

The old Celtic spirit of independence was to rise again on more than one occasion and, just as Edward II found it necessary to secure the loyalty of the Welsh people by making his son Prince of Wales, so more than one King of England had reason to remember that the Cornish were not English, seeing themselves as independent even though conquered.

19

The holy well and ancient cross at St. Cleer

THE SAINTS OF CORNWALL

Between the departure of the Romans and the arrival of the Pope's missionary, Saint Augustine, in A.D. 597, England was a pagan country, but among the Celts of Wales, Ireland, Cornwall and Brittany, Christianity continued to flourish and develop. Even so, not everybody in these western lands was a Christian. Many were totally heathen and had never heard of Christ, and many clung to the old Celtic superstitions.

There were, however, many Christian monks in the west, especially in Ireland, where there were small monasteries and learned men to teach and preach. From here, many men and women set out on missionary voyages to the other Celtic lands, carrying only a wooden cross in their hands and the knowledge of Christianity in their heads. They came to serve the people in whatever way they could and to convert them to their faith. Their task was not an easy one. They had to cross rough seas in very small boats and when they reached land they often found the people unfriendly towards them. Some were killed, others must have been too discouraged to go on, but in time their words and deeds won through.

Stories and legends about them were handed on from person to person and have come down to us, hundreds of years later, through the writings of chroniclers who often lived long after the men and women they wrote about. We do not, therefore, have a clear picture of these early Christian monks but there is enough evidence to show that they were a vital force in Cornwall in the Dark Ages. There are many Cornish towns, villages and hamlets named after them and it is obvious that they were highly thought of and that the people wanted them to be remembered. In time, they became known as saints, and Cornwall is sometimes called 'The Land of the Saints'.

Most of our parish churches are named after Celtic saints and are probably built on the spot where the original holy man had his dwelling. Saints' names in the parishes of the far west are mainly Irish in origin, those on the north coast are mainly Welsh, while in the south we find names from Brittany.

In early times it was believed that springs of water gushing from the ground were due to magic. Such places were regarded with awe and reverence. Trees also had an importance in Celtic superstition. The early Saints always tried to use these pagan superstitions to turn people towards Christian ideas and deliberately set up their crude houses and small altars on or near such 'magical' sites. They also needed water for their own use and for the all-important ceremony of baptism which accompanied conversion to Christianity. Where we find an ancient parish church in the countryside it is very likely that worship of some kind, whether Christian or pagan, has been taking place on the site for many centuries.

In Penzance, which means 'holy headland' in its original Cornish form of Pen Sans, there used to be a tiny chapel on the rocks near where the present bathing pool and the parish church of St Mary are built. St Mary's is a fairly modern church and does not have a Celtic dedication, but the site is an old one. In Bodmin the parish church of St Petroc, the largest in Cornwall, is built on the spot supposed to have been used by St Petroc and St Guron, and nearby are two little shrines marking holy wells. Tradition says that these were the sites of the original Christian churches here. At St Clether, in the heart of wooded country on the edge of Bodmin Moor, the tiny church is built in the very middle of a circular enclosure which has a ditch and a bank around it. Nearby is a holy well. It seems to be a perfect example of how the Celtic saint took over an important pagan place and used it for his own work.

Holy wells are very numerous. When the original saints lived by the springs and pools, marked now by small chapels, they had only a simple hut. It was long after their deaths that other Christians built stone walls around the wells to mark the sacred spot. Some are very crudely built, others have roofs and crosses and even gates. There is a particularly fine example at St Cleer, near Liskeard. At Madron, a mile or two from Penzance, is a holy well in which generations of small girls baptized their dolls, probably without realizing that in their play they were carrying on the tradition of centuries. In Newlyn there is still a spot known as Pin Mill where people used to throw pins into the water for good luck. No doubt it was once another holy well.

Holywell Bay, near Newquay, reminds us yet again of the early saints. Indeed, every wishing well reminds us of the early days of Christianity. We should put aside our modern superstition that throwing pins or money into a well can somehow bring good fortune, and remember the importance of water to Christians as a sign of washing away evil.

Dating also from these centuries, the sixth to the ninth approximately, are hundreds of stone crosses. Many of them began as pagan menhirs from the Megalithic Period but, with the addition of some carving, became symbols of Christianity. In some cases, a cross-piece was added to the top of the menhir instead. The carvings on the very early ones are crude, as one might expect from a sculptor with little skill and poor tools, but many of the later ones are decorated with intricate designs. The common Celtic patterns were made from interwoven lines which formed a network on the four sides of the tall base pillar. The cross itself is often in the shape of a wheel, with the four arms inside. This is called a wheel-headed Cross or, simply, a Celtic cross.

Many of the ancient crosses still stand where they were originally erected, others have been moved to the safety of churchyards. Thousands have been destroyed and there must be many gateposts in Cornwall which were once cross pillars. It is not uncommon for crosses to be discovered, serving as part of a hedge or lying in some bramble-covered ditch. When such finds are made, they are usually carefully restored to something like their original state and re-erected.

An ancient cross at Minions near Liskeard, called Long Tom

Below left: **A Celtic wheel-headed cross at Cardinham near Bodmin**

Cornish crosses had several purposes. When they were made from pagan menhirs they reminded people that Christianity had been substituted for the old ways. Sometimes they marked a holy spot, sometimes they pointed the way to a nearby shrine or guided travellers to shelter and safety. One on Bodmin Moor, called Long Tom, is supposed to have been such a signpost and in Bodmin town there is a lane called Cross Lane, where once a series of crosses marked the way to church. Many Cornish towns have roads called Cross Street and there are scores of place-names containing variations of the Cornish word 'crows'=cross. Like the place-names containing 'dinas'=fort, they often require some detective work to decipher their true meaning. Some examples are, 'Park an Grouse'=Cross Field, 'Trengrouse'=Homestead by the Cross, 'Crows an Wra'=Witch's Cross.

The story of Cornish crosses, their ages, their positions and their designs is such a fascinating study that some writers have made it a lifelong work. One good book to look at is *Granite Crosses of West Cornwall* by Laura Rowe. It contains drawings of all those in the far west, with a short description of them, and shows all the variations, from the very simple, to the most noble example of the wheel-headed type.

The Church's patron saint of Cornwall is Michael the Archangel but the two Celtic saints regarded as especially important to our land are Petroc and Piran.

Petroc was Welsh and was very well known in the sixth century, not only in Cornwall but in Wales, Ireland, Brittany and the whole of south-west England. He was the son of an important chieftain but gave up his wealth and position to become a Christian monk. After studying in Ireland, he came to Cornwall about the middle of the sixth century and landed near Padstow with a company of holy men. There, he found two other monks already working, Samson and Wethinoc, and they joined forces. The name Padstow comes from the Saxon name, Petrocstow. The Celtic name for the place was Lanwethinoc.

Petroc became a great man in the Celtic church and is said to have travelled widely, even as far as India, although there is no proof of that. Churches bearing his name are to be found over a wide area. The parish church of Padstow is St Petroc's, that in Bodmin is St Petroc's, there is a small one with the same name in the main street of Exeter, and others outside Devon and England.

After many years in the Padstow area, he came to Bodmin and set up a small monastery near the present parish church. St Guron, who had been here before him, moved to the south coast, where his name is still remembered in the villages of Gorran and Gorran Haven. The two holy wells in Bodmin are dedicated to Guron and Petroc. Of the two, Guron's is cared for, while Petroc's is sadly neglected.

Petroc died in June, A.D. 564. His bones were placed in a box and kept in Bodmin Priory for hundreds of years. This seems a strange thing to us but was a common custom at that time. Since there were no photographs to act as reminders, it seemed natural to keep as holy relics some imperishable part of the person, or something he had owned or used.

Bodmin Priory was the most important monastery in the whole of the south-west. Having started as a small monastic cell in Celtic time, it grew into a number of buildings set around a large and beautiful church. The priors of Bodmin became men of power and influence and the monastery owned many acres of land elsewhere in Cornwall. St Petroc's relics were kept beneath the altar and were the object of great veneration by the monks, the townspeople and visitors from other places.

In 1177, a monk called Roger quarrelled with the prior. In anger and revenge he stole the bones and ran off with them to France. The outcry was tremendous and the king himself ordered their return, sending armed men to fetch them from the monastery there. On the way home, the rescue party met a man with an ivory box, made in Arabia, and just right for holding the relics safely. They bought it and returned to Bodmin with the new casket amid scenes of wild rejoicing.

In the sixteenth century, some four hundred years later, King Henry VIII ordered the closure of all monasteries in the country and the confiscation or sale of all their treasures. Bodmin Priory was pulled down and most of the stone sold for building. There must still be a great deal of it in or

St. Petroc's, Bodmin. This is the largest parish church in Cornwall. Outside is a pillar from the great Bodmin Priory, and the holy well of St. Guron shown in detail in the inset picture.

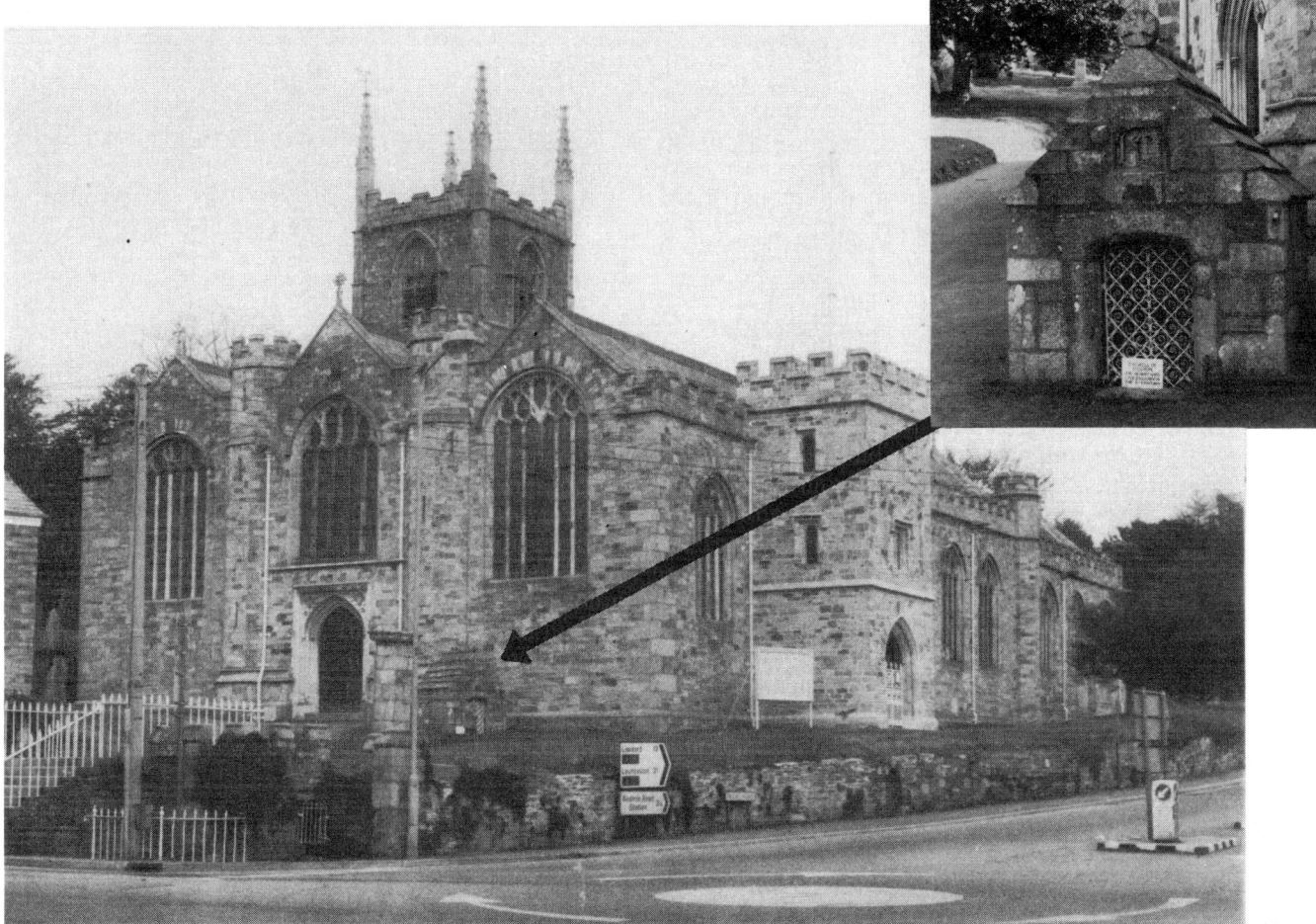

around the town but the only identifiable pieces left are a number of carved stones from the windows and doorposts. These were no good for building and were left on the site. Until recently, they lay in Bodmin's Priory Park, laid out on the monastery site, and were in danger of being destroyed or lost but they have now been assembled in one place and marked as the last surviving stones of a once famous landmark in the town. During the destruction of the priory, the tomb of one of the most famous priors, Thomas Vyvyan, was moved to the parish church across the road, and the ivory box of relics disappeared.

It was not discovered again until the eighteenth century, when some workmen making repairs in the rooms over the porch of St Petroc's Church found it bricked up in the wall. Obviously, the monks had hidden it there for safe-keeping. It was removed to the safety of a bank vault and brought out only on special occasions. A few years ago, a special resting-place was made for it in the south wall of the church and it can be seen there today, to remind us of the Celtic saint.

We know a good deal about Petroc but St Piran is a much more shadowy figure, shrouded in legend. We know that he came from Ireland and gave his name to Perranporth, Perranzabuloe, Perranwell, Perranuthnoe and Perran-ar-worthal. Legend says that his pagan enemies in Ireland threw him over a cliff with a millstone tied around his neck. By a miracle, it floated and bore him to Cornwall, where he landed at Perranzabuloe on the north coast. There is usually a grain of truth in all legends and it may be that the reference to the circular millstone really means that he came in a circular boat called a coracle. It may, however, refer to the portable altar stone carried by all early missionaries.

His relics were also kept for hundreds of years in a small chapel built among the sand dunes at Perranzabuloe. Sand dunes are always shifting and the chapel was lost beneath them. The Lost Chapel of St Piran became an object of great interest and curiosity to local people and visitors alike. Eventually, a crude tin and concrete hut was built over it to protect it from the sand. Unfortunately, many people treated it badly and it also suffered from flooding. In 1980, it was covered and sealed and is now hidden permanently from view.

Another legend says that Piran accidentally discovered the secret of extracting tin from the Cornish rocks. This is why he is the patron saint of tin-workers. He is unique among Cornish saints in that he has a special flag which has become the flag of Cornwall. It is a silver cross on a black ground and has two meanings. The silver represents the pure tin, the black stands for the raw black tin ore. The silver cross on black also stands for the victory of Christianity over evil, so we are reminded of the importance of tin to Cornwall and Piran's work as a Celtic saint.

The early Celtic saints worked in small groups and formed simple monasteries from which they carried their message into the surrounding country-side. Little trace now remains of their settlements but on the cliffs at Tintagel, close to the later castle built there, is the outline of quite a large monastery which flourished in the fifth century. There are the remains of many small buildings around the headland and excavation has shown that it was occupied by a large number of monks and that it was a place of considerable importance.

Many Cornish place-names begin with the prefix 'Lan', indicating that either monks once lived there or that the land once belonged to a monastery. There are probably as many 'Lan' names as there are saints' names.

Through the names, the old crosses, the holy wells and the legends and facts about the early Christian monks, we know that the Celtic church was a powerful force in Cornwall and the west generally, when England was pagan. From Norman times, the Celtic church and the English church journeyed together. In fact, much of the old Celtic way was lost as new ideas and practices spread from the east but here in Cornwall we can say that Christianity has been known for an unbroken period of nearly two thousand years, and we have the evidence to prove it.

Some Things To Do

1 On the Ordnance Survey maps of Cornwall, find the words:

   Menhir   Inscribed Stone   Holy Well

2 Go out and visit some of them. Draw or photo-graph them.

3 Look for Cornish crosses. Give yourself a mark for every one you find, with double marks for each wheel-headed Celtic cross.

4 Find out the name of the saint to whom your parish church is dedicated. If it is a Celtic saint, find out all you can about him or her.

5 If you live in a town or village named after a saint, find out all you can about him or her. You may have to do some detective work to find the true name as many have been altered. Thus, St Ives is named after St Ia; St Blazey after St Blaise. At Veryan, near the Lizard, the Saint is St Symphorian; at Landwednack and Towednack, the name is St Gwethnoc; and at Altarnun on Bodmin Moor, it is St Nonna or St Nun. Most churches have leaflets about their history and one of these is the best starting-point.

6 If you are very energetic, get a large sheet of paper and list every saint's name in Cornwall. When you have finished, you will know why Cornwall is called The Land of the Saints.

7 Look for the flag of St Piran as you travel around Cornwall. Draw one, or buy one for yourself and fly it on special occasions.

THE CORNISH LANGUAGE

When the invading English tribes reached the shores of the Bristol Channel in the seventh century, the Celts in Wales and those in the kingdom of Dumnonia were cut off from each other except by sea. Those in Ireland and Brittany were already separated and many of the old links between the Celtic countries were weakened or broken. In those days, when there was no radio, television, or books, a hundred miles was a long distance. It is not surprising that in the years which followed the English conquest, the language of these different Celtic peoples developed along different paths.

Because they come from the same source, there are many words, and patterns of words, which are the same in the Celtic languages. For instance, the words for the days of the week, the seasons of the year, and the basic numbers are almost identical in Welsh and Cornish. In other ways, the two languages are now so different that a Welsh speaker and a Cornish speaker cannot easily communicate with each other. These differences and likenesses also exist between Cornish and Breton, the language of Brittany.

Up to about the middle of the fourteenth century, Cornish remained the main language of Cornwall but by the start of the nineteenth century there were few who had a thorough working knowledge of their native Celtic tongue. In four hundred years English had replaced Cornish as the everyday language of trade, and the Cornish speaker had become something of a curiosity in his own land.

The use of English spread most quickly in the east, all along the banks of the Tamar and westward to Bodmin Moor. At first, it was a second language, used only in dealings with the English, who did not understand Cornish. As children grew up, with a knowledge of both English and Cornish, and as the two peoples mingled more and more, so English became the dominant speech and spread ever westward. It reached the Land's End district last of all, probably about two hundred years after it had become the working language in the east. This was because the Cornish in the distant west were remote from the mainstream of life, lived mainly in tiny hamlets and isolated cottages, and had little contact with the English.

The greatest blows to the use of Cornish came in the 16th century. We know that in 1542 most Cornish men and women were bi-lingual and there were many in the remoter areas of the west who could speak only Cornish. English, however was fast becoming the dominant language, especially in east and mid-Cornwall. A man called Andrew Borde wrote in that year:

In Cornwall is two speches, the one is naughty Englysshe, and the other is Cornysshe speche. And there be many men and women which cannot speake one word of Englysshe but all Cornysshe.

By 'naughty' English, he meant imperfect English.

In 1547, King Edward VI ordered that the Book of Common Prayer, in English, should be introduced into Cornwall and that the old Celtic customs of the church and services in Latin were to be discontinued. It is said that the first use of English in church services in Cornwall was at Menheniot in 1540, a few years before the King's decree. There was a wave of protest and a petition was sent, asking for the old language to be retained as English was not understood by many Cornish people. The King refused and a Cornish army of six thousand was raised to defend their rights. Led by Humphrey Arundell of Lanherne, and the Mayor of Bodmin, they crossed the Tamar and besieged Exeter.

When they sent the petition they stressed their loyalty to the King but, even so, their act was treasonous. It was put down by the King's men and the leaders were captured and executed. Into Cornwall came the King's officers and they searched out all those who were connected with the rebellion, and punished them very severely. If you go to St Ives, you will see the name of John Payne on the church wall. He was the chief magistrate of the town in 1549 and was hanged as a rebel. The story is told of how Bodmin's Mayor entertained the King's representative, Sir Anthony Kingston, at a very pleasant dinner, and how they had an enjoyable and friendly time together. When the dinner was over, Kingston had him taken outside and hanged for his part in the revolt.

The Prayer Book Rebellion, as it is now known, and the increasing use of English in the churches, courts and documents, spelled the end of Cornish as the language of Cornwall, except in the place-names and the dialect words still used.

In Wales, the Celtic language has survived although it is always under attack. The Welsh were allowed to have a Prayer Book printed in Welsh. Welsh is still taught in schools and is widely used, especially in the north. There are books and magazines in Welsh as well as radio and television programmes, so it is a working tongue. When English was spreading throughout Cornwall, there were few Cornish people able to read and write, and few books, so there was little support for what was only a spoken language.

Memorial to Dorothy Pentreath

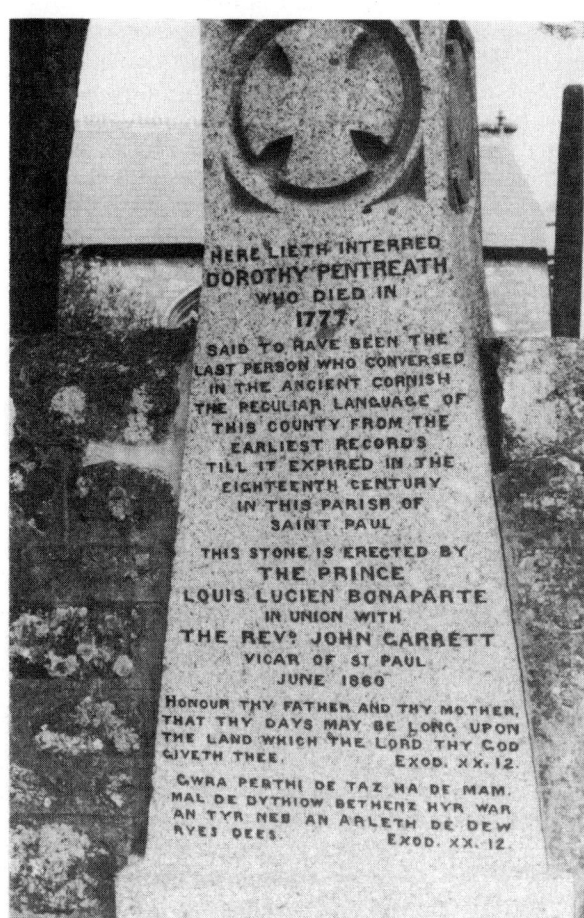

In the churchyard at Paul, near Mousehole, there is a memorial to a lady called Dorothy Pentreath who died in 1777. It says that she was the last person to speak Cornish as her native tongue. We know there were others who had some knowledge of the language after her. We do not know who was the last person to use Cornish as the main language for thinking and talking, but it is almost certain that nobody used it in that way after 1800.

Usually, when a language dies out as an everyday tongue, it never comes alive again, and a few years ago it was said that Cornish was as dead as ancient Greek. In the last few years, though, an amazing thing has happened. Many Cornish people have started to learn their language again and classes have been organized in many towns. There are now annual examinations and competitions for poetry and prose. Church services are held in Cornish at Christmas and on special occasions and, most important of all, many small children are being taught Cornish as well as English so that they will grow up to be bi-lingual. There are road and shop signs in Cornish and, generally, a great awareness of the Cornish language as something special and something to be preserved and used.

There are books of stories in Cornish, books of poetry, and Cornish song-books. An increasing number of fishing boats are given Cornish names, every major road into the Duchy now carries the name Kernow as well as the English, Cornwall; and thousands of cars carry a little plate with the word Kernow on it.

Whether we know any of the finer details of the Cornish language or not, we all use it in some way or other. Most of the place-names are Celtic and many of the personal names of people. There is a saying:

'By Tre, Pol and Pen, You shall know the Cornishmen.'

'Tre' means a home or a town or any place where people live. 'Pol' means a pool or an anchorage for ships, and 'Pen' means a headland or head. You may know somebody called Trelawny, Treneere,

The tombstone of Edwin Chirgwin, schoolmaster of St. Cleer from 1933-56. He was also a leading member of a small band of enthusiasts who revived the Cornish language fifty years ago.

Tredinnick or Polglase, Polwhele, Pender or Penhaligon, or by another name with one of these beginnings. There are thousands of place-names beginning with 'Tre', 'Pol' and 'Pen'. They are not the only Cornish names. We have already met the prefix 'Lan', meaning an enclosure and generally associated with monastic land. Another very common one is 'nan', or 'nans', or 'nance'. This means a valley and is seen in such place-names as Nanpean, Nancecuke, Nancegollan and Nanjulyan.

If you come across the name Tyack or Tyacke, it comes from the Cornish word for Farmer, 'tyak'. Angove comes from 'an gof' = the smith, and Annear was once 'an hir', meaning the long or tall person. Hayle is really the Cornish word 'heyl' = estuary, and all the words with 'eglos' in them, Treneglos, Egloskerry and Egloshayle for instance, refer to 'eglos' = church.

The study of Cornish place-names is fascinating and it is always exciting to discover the true meaning of a familiar one. There is a small reef of rocks in Mount's Bay called The Grebe and a headland by Fowey is the Gribben. At first sight, these two names have no connection and, in English, a grebe is a bird. When one discovers that the Cornish word for a reef or ledge of rock is 'gryb', it is obvious that the two places mentioned really have Cornish and not English names.

When Cornish people speak English they do so with an accent and they use many words and phrases found only in Cornwall. This is not a lack of education. In most cases, it means that the speaker is using Cornish words and patterns of speech, as a Welshman speaking English uses the sounds and patterns of his native Welsh.

Cornish speech is not the same throughout Cornwall. A man from the shores of Mount's Bay in the west does not sound the same as somebody from the mining districts of St Just, and neither sound the same as somebody from Camborne and Redruth. In the east, around Bodmin and Liskeard, there are many sounds and words which are found over the Tamar in Devon. It is common to hear somebody say 'We'm', for 'We are', in Liskeard but nobody says that in Mousehole. It shows the greater influence of English in the east.

Here are some Cornish words and phrases to learn. Most of the words are said just as they are written and, if you are Cornish by birth, the chances are that you will get them right at the first try. The only sounds which may cause difficulty at first are those of 'dh' and 'gh'. The first is always sounded as 'th' and the second is like the Scottish 'ch' as in Loch.

Onen	One	Chy	House
Deu	Two	Bal	Mine
Try	Three	Scath	Boat
Peswar	Four	Den	Man
Pymp	Five	Benen	Woman
Whegh	Six	Flogh	Child
Seyth	Seven	Mam	Mother
Eth	Eight	Tas	Father
Naw	Nine	Cath	Cat
Dek	Ten	Ky	Dog
		Porth	Harbour
Gwyn	White	Avon	River
Du	Black	Mor	Sea
Glas	Blue	Forth	Road
Ruth	Red	Steren	Star
Gwer	Green	Ebren	Sky
Melen	Yellow	Bre	Hill

Onen hag Oll   One and All (The Cornish motto)
Kernow   Cornwall
Kernow bys vyken   Cornwall for ever
Kernow kensa   Cornwall first

Fishing boats at Newlyn with names in the Cornish language. 'Tyak Mor' means Farmer of the Sea, and 'Leven-Mor' means, approximately, Smooth Sea.

Some Things To Do

1 Look for Cornish names in the telephone directory under Tre, Pol and Pen.

2 Make a list of all the Cornish place-names near where you live and try to find out their meaning.

3 Look out for Cornish signs.

4 Find out where you can learn Cornish.

5 Using the words on the previous page, make some drawings and write the Cornish words underneath them.

Chons da — Good luck!

SOME MORE CORNISH WORDS

Look at the Cornish words on page 27

Morvoren (mermaid)

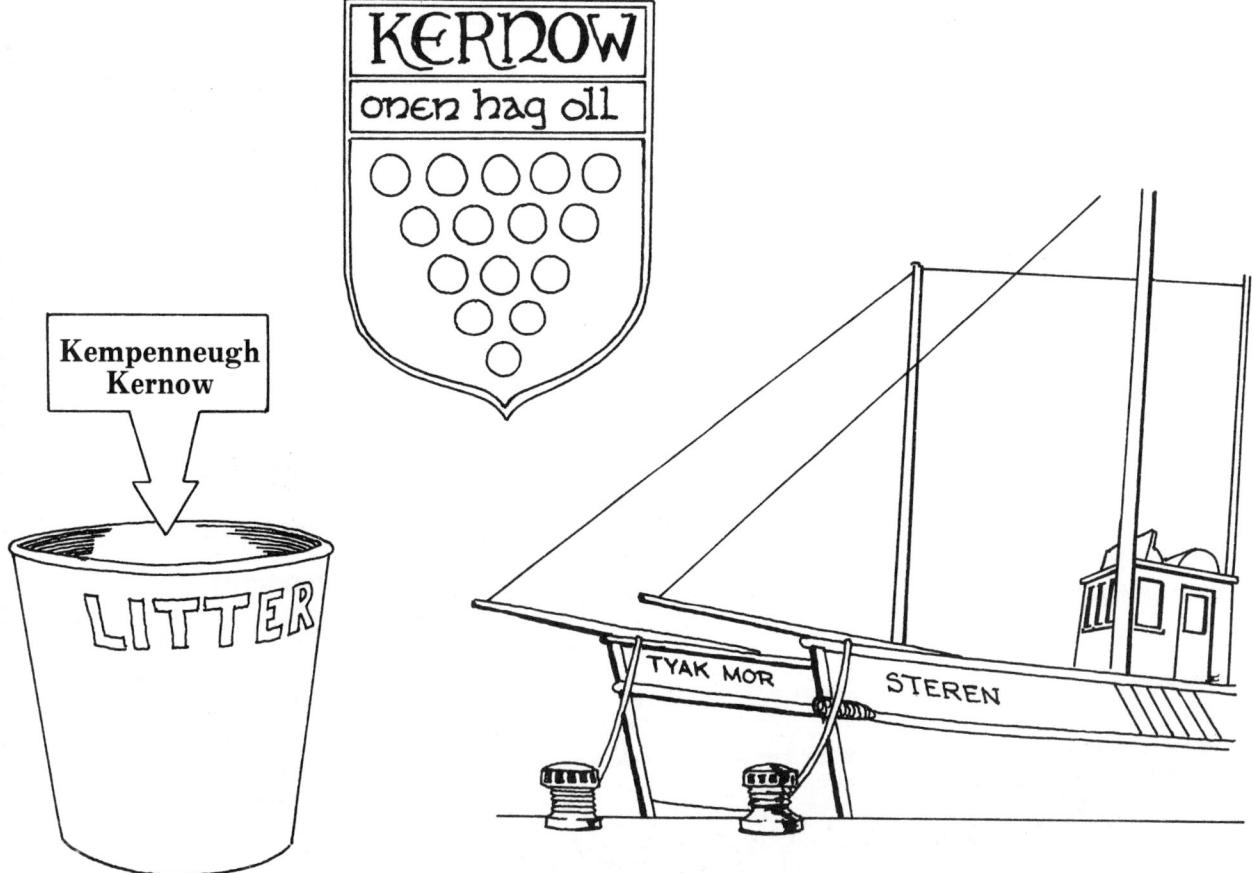

Keep Cornwall tidy

TYAK MOR (glas)   STEREN (melen)
colour the boats

28

WRITE THE CORNISH WORDS UNDER THESE PICTURES

house

. . . .

cat

. . . .

dog

. . . .

tin mine

. . . .

three

. . . .

six

. . . .

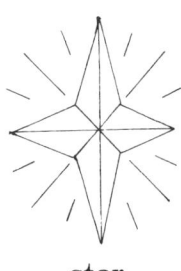

star

. . . .

woman

. . . .

boat

. . . .

child

. . . .

road

. . . .

seven

. . . .

CORNISH TIN MINING

Early tin-workers dug the ore from the surface, or washed it from the mud and sand of river beds

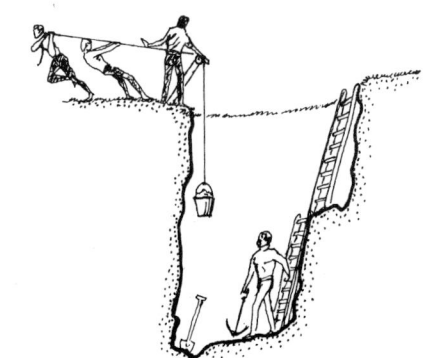

Then they went down, deeper and deeper...

...until there was a maze of tunnels and shafts below the ground

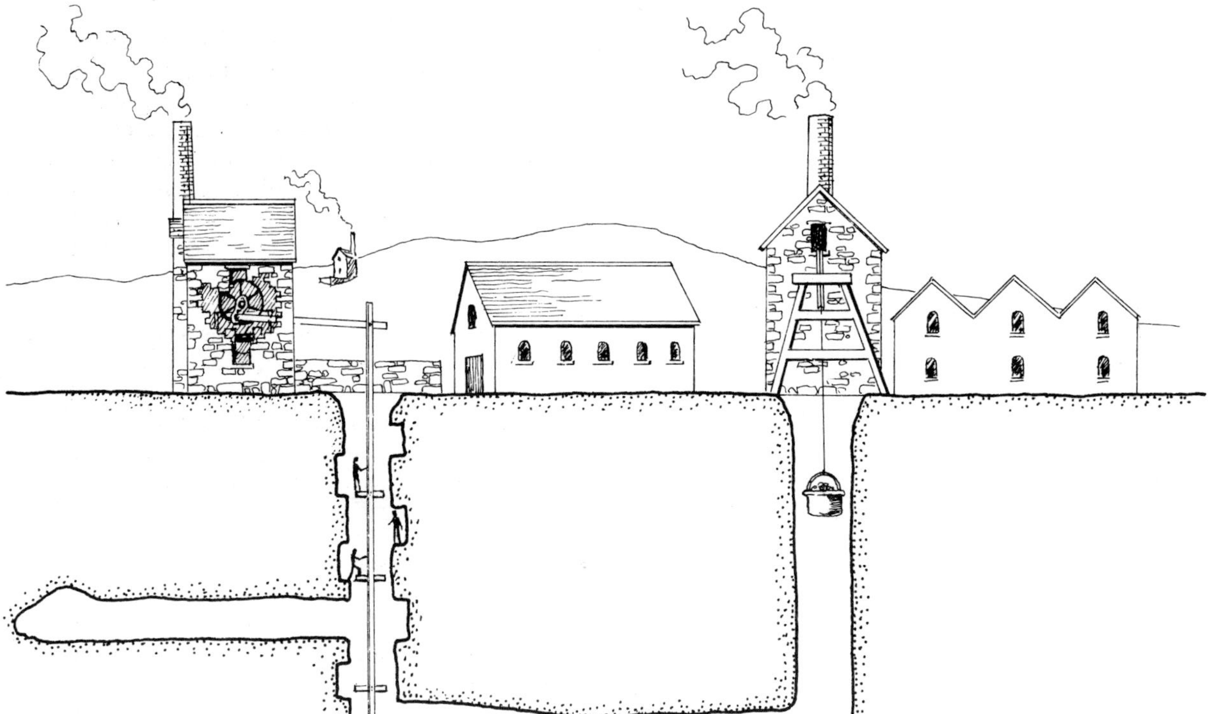

Chapter 5

MINES AND MINERS OF CORNWALL

We do not know when Man first discovered the secrets of extracting metals from certain rocks or how he developed his knowledge into a skilful science. We think that metal-working began in the lands around the Mediterranean, somewhere about 4000 B.C.

Bronze Age settlers in Cornwall found good supplies of tin ore and, as we have read, they began to organize a trade in the ore and in articles made from tin. Skills were learned by experiment and there must have been many trials and failures before it was discovered exactly how to mix tin and copper to produce good, hard-wearing bronze. We can be sure that the ancient miners and smiths guarded their secrets very carefully and that they were passed on only to a worthy few.

Cornwall became known to merchants far beyond its own shores and is mentioned in a number of very old writings as being rich in mineral wealth. A well-known port in ancient times was called Ictis and some historians have identified it with St Michael's Mount, near Penzance. Some of the descriptions fit the Mount and the bay in which it stands, but other experts claim that Ictis was farther along the English Channel. Whatever the truth, it is certain that traders from the Mediterranean and the Atlantic coast of Spain sailed their ships hundreds of miles to Cornwall. There are stories that the regular traders tried hard to keep their destination secret, so as to keep as much profit to themselves as they could. A story says that one ship's captain ran his vessel ashore in an attempt to shake off a following merchant.

The early tin-workers found ores on the slopes of the hills, and along the banks of streams where fine particles had been washed into the mud and gravel. They had no tools to dig deep into the ground so they were not miners in the modern sense of the word. Where they found lumps of tin-bearing rock, laboriously they crushed them with hammers, and collected tiny fragments from the river beds through washing the silt in sieves, a process called 'streaming'.

After repeated washings, enough powder was collected to be smelted, that is, turned to liquid by means of fire in a kiln. By pouring the molten metal into moulds it could be turned into axe heads, arrow and spearheads and jewellery.

As time progressed, and we are talking in terms of centuries, men were able to follow the rich veins of ore, 'lodes', farther underground. They had better tools with which to dig and to break up the hard granite and skilled knowledge to show them the best sites. Real mining, with shafts and tunnels underground, did not begin until the fourteenth and fifteenth centuries.

The two great problems which limited progress for hundreds more years were, the support of the sides of the shafts and the roofs of the tunnels, and the disposal of the water which collected in the workings. Water is always seeping down through the ground and many of the best places for mining were very wet. Small amounts could be baled out, using canvas or wooden buckets, and there were devices operated by a horse or ox walking round and round in a circle at the surface, constantly raising buckets and tipping them into a nearby stream or wooden channel. Such devices are still used today in Africa and the Far East. Large amounts of timber were needed for supports in the mine and, just as important, the engineering knowledge to build them correctly to take the enormous stresses.

The invention of the steam-engine in the eighteenth century and its rapid development in the nineteenth century revolutionized all mining. An engine could be used to operate pumps at a great depth, it could haul up waste and ore from the shafts, and machinery at the surface could do many of the jobs previously done by hand. The engineer and the inventor became important men. They were, in their day, what the modern rocket engineer and space scientist are in our time.

There was fierce competition between engineers to see who could make the best engines to do the most efficient work using the least amount of fuel. The names of Watt, Boulton and Newcomen became famous throughout the land and, in Cornwall, our own great mining engineer Richard

31

Trevithick, made an enormous contribution to mining progress.

So, aided by steam power, mines went ever deeper. On the slopes, horizontal tunnels, adits, were dug to assist the drainage and, below ground, mines became a network of tunnels. Some were worked for ore, some were used for the transport of materials, some were for ventilation and many were started and abandoned when the ore ran out. On the surface, or 'at grass' as the miners called it, buildings were erected in stone, wood and corrugated iron. The ground quickly became littered with engine-houses, stables, sheds of all kinds, heaps of waste and building materials. Mines were not things of beauty and in those days there were no planning regulations. They were working places, devoted entirely to the raising of minerals from the earth, processing them as far as possible and shipping the results as quickly as possible to the ports.

There was work for everybody, men, women and even young children. Many of the above-ground tasks were done by women, who were known as 'bal-maidens' and small children could fetch and carry and do odd jobs. Boys around twelve years old joined their fathers underground and, as the mines grew larger and more prosperous in the early nineteenth century, mining became a family tradition in the main mining areas of West Penwith, Camborne-Redruth and Liskeard. It is in these upland areas that the great granite rock masses yield the largest amounts of tin and copper. There were by-products: lead was also found, and arsenic was collected from the waste products. Very little was wasted.

By our standards, life for the miner and his family was very hard. Cottages were tiny, perhaps with only one room and a sleeping loft among the rafters for the children. Water had to be fetched from the local pump and there were, of course, no bathrooms or taps within the house. A garden provided the bulk of the food in summer, with potatoes being the staple item. Most miners kept a few chickens and a cow, to provide eggs and milk. On the coast, there were fish to catch and it was not unusual for several men to have shares in a small boat and to lay nets and crab-pots.

Looking after the garden, the animals and going fishing were spare time occupations. When we consider the length of the miners' working day and the arduous nature of the work, we can only marvel at their energy and wonder that they could possibly be the same kind of people as ourselves. There were three eight-hour shifts in the mines daily. Known as cores, they were worked from six in the morning, two in the afternoon and ten at night. Many men walked up to five miles to a mine from their homes and, after climbing down hundreds of yards of vertical ladders, walked a further mile or two to where they actually began work. The reverse happened after eight hours of back-breaking labour in hot, cramped and frequently wet conditions.

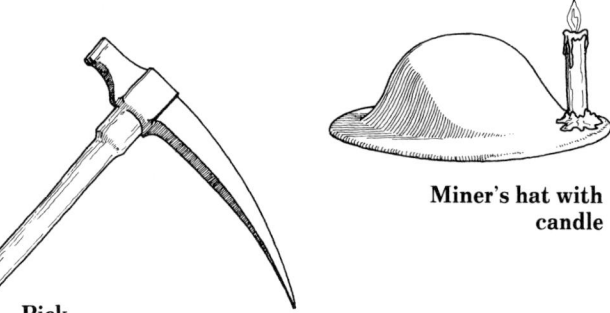

Pick

Miner's hat with candle

Chisels and borers   **Heavy hammer**

However many improvements were made to the machinery, tunnels and shafts still had to be dug by hand. It is in this work that the skill of the Cornish miner was best seen. The rock was very hard and they had to cut their way through with chisels called gads, hammers and the assistance of dynamite. Miners often worked in pairs, one holding and turning the gad, the other striking it with a sledgehammer. A good team could cut quite long stretches in a day and in the mining world, Cornish 'hard-rock' men were in great demand wherever strength, stamina and skill were wanted.

Underground, it was pitch black except for the pools of light thrown by the candles stuck to the front of the canvas hats or placed on ledges on the walls. Men bought their candles and tools and, when pay day came, they were often in debt for them to the mine owner. There were several ways of earning money but generally a miner was paid according to the quality and quantity of good ore brought to the surface. If he were fortunate and had a dry, workable pitch with rich lodes, he could earn a living wage. If, on the other hand, he found himself with a difficult pitch, where the lode was patchy and of poor quality, he took home very little.

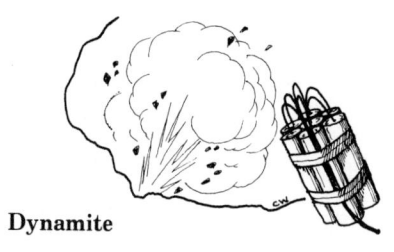

Dynamite

There was always danger. Rocks fell from the roofs, tunnels caved in, explosions sometimes caused disasters, and rotten ladders and planks threw many a miner to his death into deep holes and shafts.

Medical services were primitive and expensive. A miner too badly injured to continue to work had to rely on charity. Every mining village had its little band of cripples sitting forlornly in the village square as a grim reminder of the cost of tin and copper.

And yet they were generally cheerful. At a time when all life was hard, they did not consider themselves as being any worse off than most. They sang as they went to and from work. They sang while they worked, and on Sundays they sang lustily in the churches and chapels. They had a natural ability to harmonize and the sound of scores of men singing favourite hymns in harmony as they made their way over the downs and along the roads and paths is something well remembered by the older people of Cornwall.

Climbing up and down miles of ladders was exhausting and engineers eventually invented the man-engine, a mechanical lift in the shaft. The first one in Cornwall was introduced in 1841. It had a vertical rod the length of the shaft which moved upwards and downwards about twelve feet every time the flywheel of the steam engine turned. There were fixed platforms on the rod and on the sides of the shaft. Miners stepped from one platform to the other either as the rod went upwards, to get to the surface, or downwards if they wanted to descend. Man-engines saved much effort but care was needed and many of the young men scorned their use, preferring to race their friends on the ladders or to ride on the ore buckets. The last man-engine in use was at the great Levant Mine, near St Just in Penwith. In 1919 the rod broke and plunged to the bottom of the shaft, killing thirty-one men and boys. This was a tragedy to the villages of St Just, Pendeen and Trewellard, many families losing several members. All the churchyards in the district bear witness to this and other disasters, such as the one in nearby Wheal Owles where a number of miners were drowned as they accidentally penetrated flooded and abandoned workings.

Many miners believed in underground ghosts. It was not hard to imagine spirits in the dim flickering light and to hear ghostly knockings. They said it was the Bucca, the spirit of the mine, or the 'Old Men', still looking for minerals after many centuries. There was a custom of leaving the corner of a pasty for the spirit, to keep him happy.

There are also many stories of miners refusing to go to work on a particular day because they feared a disaster. In some cases, the warnings proved to be well-founded, an accident occurring just where the man would have been working.

When the ore was smelted into blocks or ingots, it was tested for quality and stamped with an official mark and the owner's name. This was done in one of five towns, Liskeard, Lostwithiel, Truro, Helston or Penzance. The work was called coinage and the towns, coinage towns. In most of them, you will still find streets called Coinagehall Street. All the work of the mines was governed by a strict set of rules called Stannary Law and for hundreds of years all miners had to obey them or be fined. Because of the importance of their work, miners also had special privileges, many of them dating back centuries. Stannary Law has never actually been cancelled by Parliament and some people still claim the old privileges and rights.

The Crowns section of Botallack Mine, St. Just.
A shaft and tunnel went out far under the sea.
This was one of the last mines to close.
It was also one of the richest,
and is now being re-explored.

The prosperity of the Cornish mines was at its greatest between about 1850 and 1865. Most of the world's supply of tin and copper came from Cornwall and there was no shortage of people willing to invest money in new ventures. When the price of metals was high, they could be assured of a high return. Unfortunately, many mines were not well managed and when difficulties arose, investors often withdrew their cash. If a mine owner had to spend months searching for fresh lodes, without getting any profit, money often ran out, resulting in closure, flooding and unemployment.

Although mining for tin is usually thought to have been the main occupation in Cornwall, more money was made from copper. Many mines began as tin workings and changed to copper mining when veins of that mineral were found below the tin lode. In some cases, tin was again discovered below the copper. After the great boom, Cornish mines fell on hard times. Many closed through lack of money or lack of good-quality ores. In the middle of the nineteenth century, enormous deposits of tin and copper were discovered abroad. Deep mining was not needed to get it, and with cheap labour available, it was less expensive to buy it abroad and to carry it vast distances to this country than to mine it at home.

Struggling Cornish mines could no longer compete and the mining districts became desolate and derelict. The pumps stopped, water rose in the workings and the machinery rusted. What were the miners to do? There was no other work. There was no money for rent, food and clothes and in those days there was no government help.

There were mines in America, Australia, South America, South Africa and Malaya and the skilled Cornishman was always welcome there. So began a great emigration. Thousands of young men left Cornwall for a new life overseas and the newspapers were full of advertisements for cheap passages, with the promise of well-paid work at the end of them. Many small villages lost most of their men. They became ghost towns, with only the occasional letter to give news of husbands and sons. There was no news at all from hundreds and they vanished from their families as if they had never existed. Most never came home again. Some sent for wives and children, many others told their male relatives to come out and join them.

In the new lands, Cornishmen tended to stick together and it seemed to the people already living there that all Cornishmen were related. When they built houses, chapels and schools, they did so in the Cornish style and their speech set them apart as a different race. They earned the nickname of Cousin Jack and it was said that wherever there was a hole in the ground in any part of the world, there was sure to be a Cousin Jack at the bottom of it. There are still communities in America, South Africa and Australia which cling strongly to their Cornish heritage and in which the common names are Pengelly, Trembath, Polkinghorne, Jago, Glasson and Pollard. In Australia, near Adelaide, there is a copper mining town called Moonta. A large signboard says, 'Moonta,

Australia's Little Cornwall', and the now-ruined engine-houses there are exactly like those seen in Cornwall.

Some miners did return, often having made money. In every mining district of Cornwall there are houses named Kimberley, Nevada House, Arizona and Bute, reminders of the Cornish miner abroad.

Local newspapers in Cornwall frequently carry letters from America and Australia, asking for information about ancestors. Usually, the writers know little about their origins except that their great-grandfathers once lived in a particular town or village and emigrated in a certain year. Interest in the members of the family who came from Cornwall is strong, and the letter-writers want to know more about them, how they lived in Cornwall and exactly where they lived.

Although Cornish mining has now almost died out, the ruins of a once busy industry can still be seen. The old engine-houses point to the sky and, in the main mining districts, they cluster thickly around old shafts, crumbling granite walls and heaps of waste material. Exploring them is interesting but can also be very dangerous. Some shafts are unfenced and all are very deep. To fall into one is fatal and if the unfortunate person is alone, he could well disappear for ever. Only a few of the great engines have been preserved. The best may be seen at Pool, Camborne. In a wonderfully-preserved engine-house is the last beam winding-engine in Cornwall, made at the Holman Foundry in Camborne in 1887. Nearby are two other beam engines, preserved for all time.

East Pool Engine-house

The ruins of Wheal Peevor near Redruth

The old mines were given strange names. A large number begin with the Cornish word 'whel' = tin mine, written in the English fashion as wheal. The names were sometimes hopeful, sometimes fanciful and often the names of men and women associated with the owners, or famous at the time.

Here are some examples:

Wheal Busy
Wheal Cunning
Wheal Fortune
Wheal Freedom
Wheal Providence
Wheal Alfred
Wheal Kitty
Wheal Sisters
Wheal Chance
Wheal Betsy
Wheal Hope
Wheal Buller
Ding Dong
Great Work
East Wheal Strawberry

Cook's Kitchen
Ting Tang
Perran Great St George

A handful of mines have survived. Geevor and South Crofty, at Pendeen and Camborne, have worked continuously since the last century and have taken over some of the old workings next to them. At Geevor, the former Levant workings are being reworked, and the undersea part of Levant has been de-watered. Wheal Jane was restarted near Redruth but has had a troubled history because of the high cost of development and the varying cost of tin. Modern mining requires vast sums of money and, unless the price of tin is high, costs soon outstrip profits. Experiments are going on in various parts of the Duchy and it may be that one day we shall see new mines being started and old ones reopened. They will, however, seem less romantic than the old ones as we shall no longer see the tall chimneys belching black smoke into the sky and the great beams moving up and down in their work It will all be tidy and the planners will make sure that the buildings blend into the landscape.

**The headgear at South Crofty,
a mine that is still working**

One kind of mining still thrives in Cornwall, the quarrying of china clay. About the year 1755, a man called Thomas Cookworthy found a material of this name in the pleasant fields around St Austell.* It was called 'china' clay because it is supposed to have been originally discovered in China, where it was used to make fine porcelain. It is formed from felspar, a constituent of granite. Its proper name is Kaolin, which is the name given to the 'white mountain' in China where this type of clay was first mined.

When extracted from the broken-down granite it is pure-white, soft clay. Cookworthy quickly and quietly bought much of the land where he found it and began an industry for quarrying it.

*Cookworthy first discovered china clay at Tregonning Hill, Breage.

Two views of the china clay workings

In the slate country of North Cornwall is the huge quarry of Delabole, at one time the largest slate quarry in the land. Millions of tons of slate have been turned into roofing slates, gravestones and paving slabs. Again, cheaper materials are now used for these purposes, although the National Trust keeps several men employed at making traditional roofing slates for the repair of their older properties.

Times change and people have to change with the times. In the past, much of Cornwall's wealth has come from the ground. We have provided the world with tin, copper and other minerals, with china-clay, with stone for its roads and with slate for its buildings. The world still needs some of our wealth and perhaps the day will come, when times change again, when it will be asking for more.

Since then, the whole St Austell district has been turned into a series of enormous pits and dumps. The dumps can be seen for miles and they were known as the Cornish Alps because they shone in the sunlight and looked like pointed mountains. In recent years they have been flattened because of fears for the safety of those living in their shadow, only one or two remaining as landmarks.

The clay is dug out by mechanical diggers or washed out by high-pressure hoses. Mixed with sand and grit, it settles in large tanks where it is separated from the waste. The pure clay is then removed and dried into powder.

The bulk of the china clay is taken away from Cornwall by sea, from the ports of Fowey, Par and Charlestown. It is used in the manufacture of paper and cosmetics and pottery-ware. It is a very valuable mineral and the St Austell area owes its prosperity to it. One cannot say that the china clay works are beautiful. The countryside is scarred and laid bare and a white dust lies over everything. But the industry is an economic necessity and gives employment to thousands of men and women all over the world. Just as mining was a family job when tin and copper mines were at their peak, so, in St Austell, there are families where the men have always been clayworkers.

Granite is a hard rock and for centuries it has been used for building. When it is cut and shaped by skilled masons it can be polished to look like marble. Wherever you go in Cornwall you will see it, in the older schools, churches, public buildings, houses and hotels. It is now very expensive to use, as its preparation takes such a long time, so most of our new buildings use cheaper materials such as bricks or concrete blocks. Many of the latter are made from the waste grit of the china-clay industry. Other rocks in Cornwall provide stone for road-making and wherever one drives, in this country or abroad, it is quite likely that Cornish roadstone has been used in the highway.

Some Things To Do

1 Visit the Poldark Mine and Tolgus Tin in mid-Cornwall to see mines in action and models of the old industry.

2 Visit some old ruined workings but be very careful. Shafts and ruined buildings can be dangerous.

3 If there are old workings where you live, find out their names and what you can about their history.

4 If you live in a mining area, examine the names of the older houses and see if you can find any from overseas, from the U.S.A., South Africa or Australia.

5 Visit the restored engine-house at East Pool, Camborne.

6 Visit the R.I.C. Museum at Truro and look at the mining exhibits there.

Chapter 6

CORNISH FISHERMEN

Fishing has been as important to Cornwall as mining, and it has been carried on ever since man first arrived here. Like mining, it grew from small beginnings into a flourishing industry. Just as mining development was revolutionized by the coming of the steam-engine, so Cornish fishing was revolutionized by the coming of the railway. Harbours were connected to the great cities where there were teeming millions eager to buy cheap fish. For the first time it was possible for fish caught off Cornwall in the early hours of the morning to be on sale in London the same day.

In the second half of the nineteenth century, the Cornish fishing industry employed thousands of boats and tens of thousands of women and men. There was also plenty of work for those looking after the boats and providing equipment and food. After the Great War of 1914-18, fishing began to decline. There were many reasons. The most important fish, pilchards, changed their seasonal migrations and were no longer found in such enormous numbers. Deepwater trawlers from the large ports on England's east coast brought back huge catches of fish from the cold waters around the Arctic Circle, and supplies of cheap canned fish from abroad increased. There was also a falling-off in the demand for salted pilchards from such countries as Italy and Spain.

So, Cornwall's fishing industry grew smaller. Boats were laid up and sold and young men turned to other, easier work. Many fishermen found that it was more profitable to sell fishing and pleasure trips to holidaymakers, and to turn their homes into guest houses. In most of Cornwall's little harbours and coves today, there is only a handful of small boats working and at present there seems little hope of any improvement. But, as with mining, times change and we may yet see great things.

The very first people caught fish for their own use and did not venture far away from the safety of the shore. Most of their fishing was done in rivers and from the rocks. Later, when life became more settled and people began to live in villages, there must have been men who not only caught

fish for themselves but for others as well, exchanging what they did not want for their own families for useful articles and other kinds of food.

Still later, when boats were larger and men were no longer afraid to sail far out to sea, there were those who became full-time fishermen and set up their homes by the water's edge. They became skilled in the various ways of ensnaring fish, in the design of boats, sails and nets.

We know that the Cornish fishermen were important as far back as the days of King John for he made laws about the catching and selling of fish. In those days it was difficult to keep the catches fresh. There were no refrigerators and no ice, except in the coldest of winters, and even then the quantity available was too small to be important. The usual way of keeping fish fresh was by sprinkling it with salt, a scarce and valuable item. You may remember that in biblical days salt was one of the most valuable possessions and the man who had a plentiful supply was considered to be rich. We still hear the expression that somebody is, or is not, 'worth his salt'. In medieval times, it was the custom to place a bowl of salt in the middle of the table so that those sitting round it could dip their food into it, Those of higher rank sat at one end of the table and the less important sat at the other end, above and below the salt.

In Cornwall, fishermen used to collect seawater in shallow ponds on the shore, allowing the sun to evaporate the water, leaving a small crust of salt to be scraped off. It was a poor way but the only one available. You will still find some places near fishing villages, named 'Saltponds'.

The speed at which fish went bad limited its use and for centuries catches were sold within a few miles of where they were caught. Donkey carts toured the country villages and towns and many men and women walked from house to house, carrying fish in a basket on their backs and crying their wares as they went. At one time, as many as a hundred pilchards could be bought for a penny.

The travelling salesmen and women were a familiar and colourful sight all round the coasts. They were called 'jowsters'. The women wore an

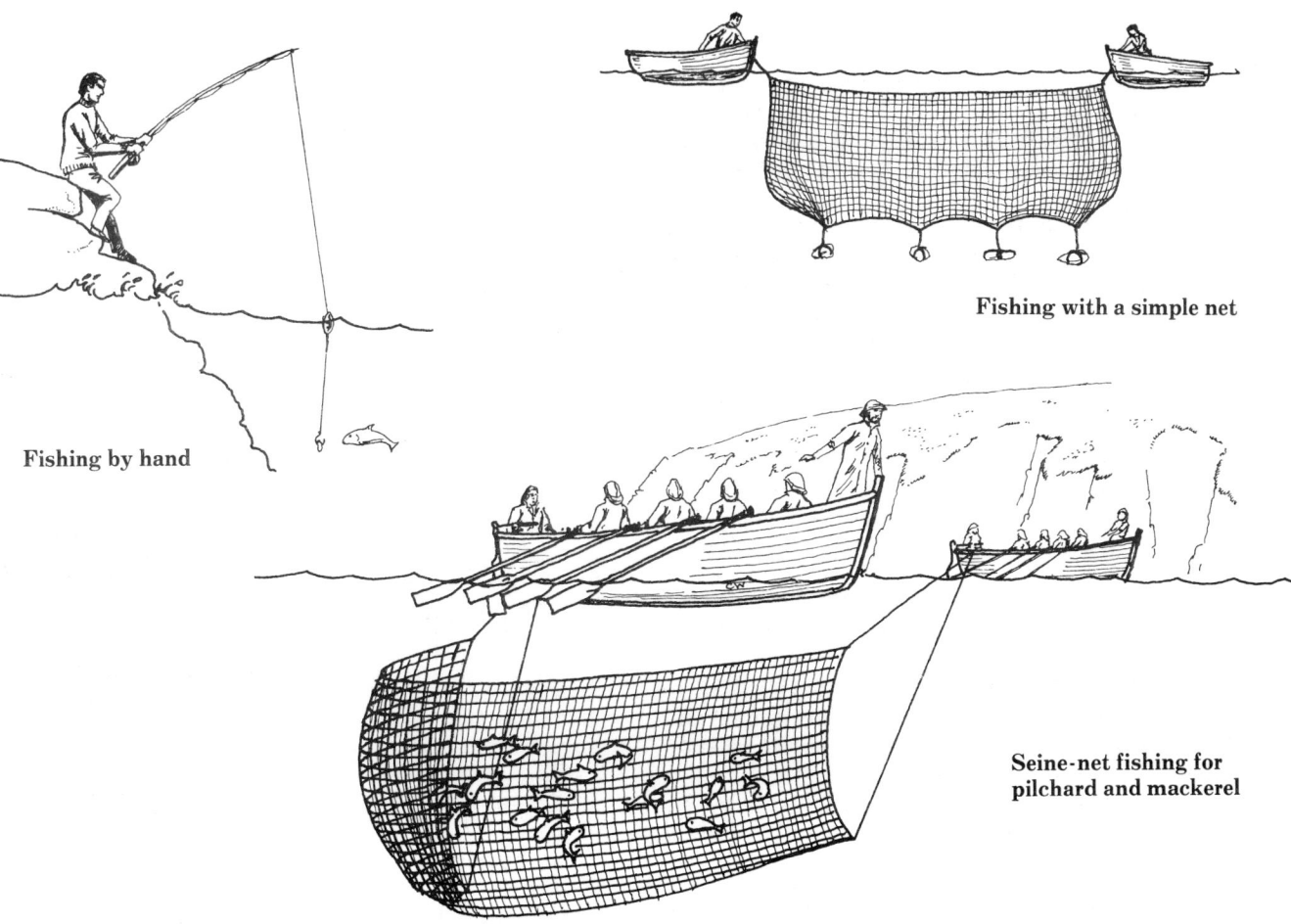

Fishing by hand

Fishing with a simple net

Seine-net fishing for pilchard and mackerel

easily recognizable uniform, red jacket, blue serge skirt, white apron, buckled shoes and a large broad-brimmed hat. They carried their fish in a basket called a 'cowel', a Cornish word for a flat, open pannier.

The railway bridge across the Tamar at Saltash was opened in 1859, making Cornwall far more accessible and ushering in the boom years of Cornish fishing.

Around harvest time every year, enormous shoals of pilchards containing millions of fish used to appear off the south-west coast. During the weeks before Christmas they got closer and closer to the shore. Their time of arrival was so predictable that watchers, known as 'huers' used to keep look-out from the cliffs. From high up, the shoals could be seen as a dark stain on the water, and the experienced huer was able to estimate the size of the shoal and the direction in which it was moving.

While they were still some way from land, the fish were caught in nets. The boats would leave harbour early in the evening and shoot their nets as it was getting dark. They would then drift with their nets stretching perhaps a mile from them and the crews would snatch a few hours sleep. In the early hours the fishermen would haul in the catch and empty vast quantities of silvery pilchards into their boats. As soon as the fish were safely on board, the boats would race for the harbour. The first boat to land the catch got the best price so there was great competition. Boat-builders vied with each other to build boats that were both seaworthy and fast.

The Cornish fishing lugger was about thirty or forty feet long, and broad beamed. It had a straight stem and stern and carried two short masts, each with one or two canvas sails. The sails were hung on long poles called yards and were shifted from one side of the mast to the other in accordance with the direction of the wind. The earliest luggers had three masts but, by the 1880s, the two-masted vessel was general. Many had no decks or cabins but were open for their entire length. As the century progressed, decking was provided and a wheelhouse, with a small cabin underneath.

We are used to seeing yachts with sleek, graceful lines and beside these fishing boats do not look fast. In light winds or in gales they could move swiftly, however, and fishermen took a great pride in the sailing qualities of their craft, holding races against each other to show their skill.

There are a few good models in the R.I.C Museum at Truro which show what they were like. One lugger is still sailing, the former St Ives boat, Barnabas, which has been restored and preserved.

When the shoals came close inshore, there was a different method of catching the fish, Every fishing cove and port had large rowing boats, seine-boats, which carried a very large and specially-shaped net. It was usual to divide the offshore waters into 'stems', each one being the property of one or more teams. Seiners worked in groups of three boats, the largest being the seine-boat proper and the smaller ones being used to carry the ends of the net around the shoal and encircle it.

The taking of a shoal by the seiners was a time of tremendous excitement. At the first cry from the huer, the entire village would rush to the beach, the men to launch the seine-boats, the women and children to watch and to shout encouragement, and to prepare for the busy work of scooping the fish into baskets. As the net was drawn around the fish, the fishermen would shout and beat the water with oars to drive the fish deeper and deeper into the trap. Eventually, the struggling millions would be drawn to the beach where the receding tide would leave them high and dry.

The huer, from his vantage point, would direct the boats by waving branches of furze (gorse) tied to poles and a great deal depended on his skill. His famous cry of 'Hevva! Hevva!' is still remembered in many Cornish homes where 'heavy cake' is made. This is a flat dough cake with currants and sugar and 'heavy' does not refer to its weight but to the cry of the huer, who often carried a good supply of it in his pocket. At some places around the coast, there are huers' huts still to be seen. They remind us of the days when they gave some shelter to the sentry there.

After the pilchards moved away from the coast in their annual migration, the larger boats joined in the herring fishing in Ireland, and later moved around the north of Scotland and down the east coast to fishing ports such as Whitby and Scarborough. Cornish boats and Cornish fishermen were as well known there as they were at home. At Whitby every year there was a regatta for fishing craft and Newlyn boats always took part and won many prizes.

**Mount's Bay sailing lugger
(no longer seen)**

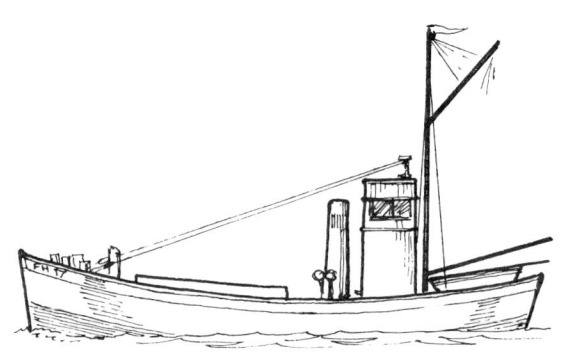

'Pilchard driver'

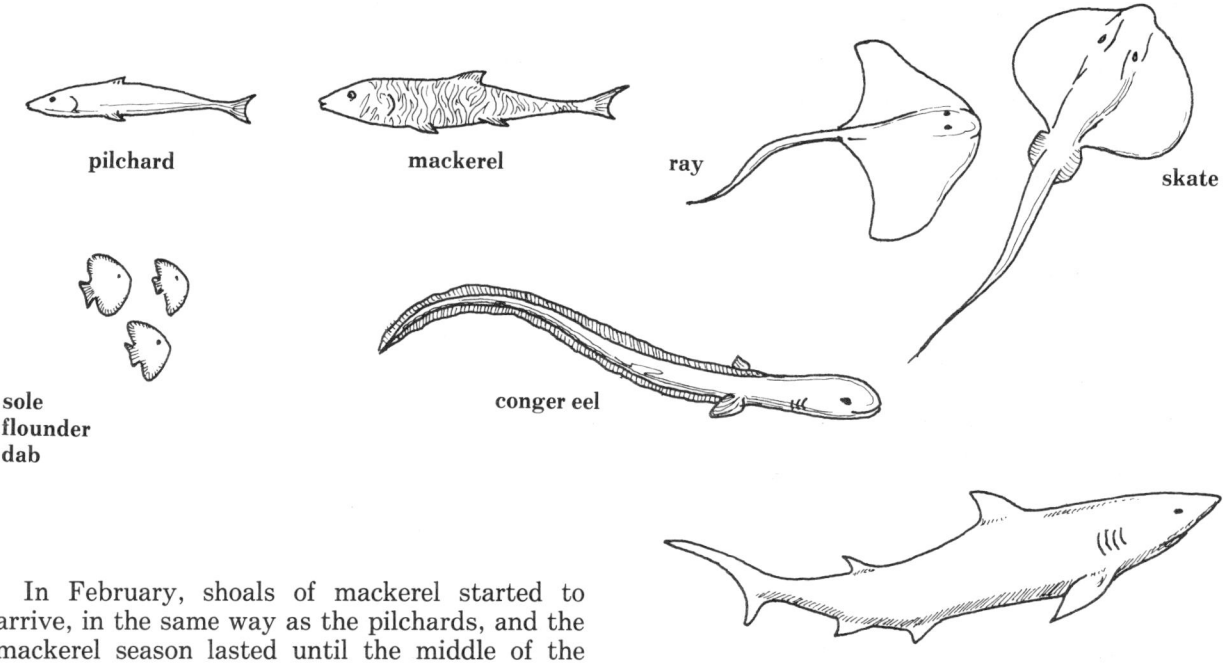

pilchard   mackerel   ray   skate

sole
flounder   conger eel
dab

shark

In February, shoals of mackerel started to arrive, in the same way as the pilchards, and the mackerel season lasted until the middle of the summer. The same methods of catching were used

39

East Coast steam drifters in Newlyn about 1900

and scores of drifters from the east coast ports also came to join in. At Newlyn, the principal harbour, there were hundreds of boats at the height of the season, and the local children knew them all by name and could identify them even when they were a long way out in the bay.

Towards the end of the century, an increasing number of boats had engines and many of the east coast drifters were fitted with coal-fired steam-engines. The sailing luggers had engines installed and a large number were still around well into this century, minus their sails and unrecognisable as former sailing craft to the landsman's eye.

All these boats needed nets, baskets, ropes, repairs, paraffin, candles and food, and the steamers required huge supplies of coal to keep them going. The visiting fishermen needed beds and meals, as few of them slept on their boats if it could be avoided. Newlyn was an incredibly busy port, with almost everybody involved in fishing or in supplying the needs of fishermen. Even in the 1930s, Newlyn boasted many grocers' shops, butchers, ships' chandlers, coal stores. Newlyn housewives often earned extra money by letting rooms to the east coast men.

The preservation of fish was still a problem and, before ice was made locally, blocks of it were brought in ships all the way from Norway. The newspaper, *The Cornishman*, for 4 May, 1896, talking about the arrival of five hundred tons of ice in the Norwegian barque *Glommen*, said this:

All one can see in Newlyn are busy horses drawing empty boxes, straw, ice and fish, and the pier packed with boxes. East Coast men mingle with Mount's Bay men in the busy, excited crowd of fishermen, buyers, packers and a thousand others.

The horses were so busy and their drivers so anxious not to miss the fish train from Penzance that the newspapers of the time are full of reports of court cases, where drivers are charged with 'furious driving'.

Fish was also sent abroad to the mainly Catholic countries of Italy and Spain, where the laws of their religion forbade the eating of meat on certain days in the year. Here fish was in great demand. This was before the days of canning in metal tins. Pilchards can be preserved for a long time if they are treated in the right way. In Cornwall they were taken to fish cellars and were packed in layers round the walls. Each layer was sprinkled with salt and pressed down with heavy stones, squeezing out the oil and blood. As the pile sank, more and more layers were added until there was a mass of tightly compressed fish. They were then packed into barrels and stored to await the arrival of a steamer.

Although the method is no longer used, the old fish cellars still stand, doing modern service as garages or workshops, or even restaurants. In many of them, the tanks still stand against the walls and often one sees cottage gardens edged with the old pressing-stones. Pickling in brine was also used and the smoking of mackerel was first done in Tudor times. Having died out, it has recently returned and smoked mackerel has become a delicacy in hotels throughout the country.

Nothing from the pilchard catch was wasted. The oil and blood were collected, refined and sold. Oil was used in lamps and farmers used the cellar sweepings as manure. When pilchards could be bought very cheaply, Cornish housewives 'marinated' them, by putting them in flat dishes

40

Above and below: Two early photos of Newlyn

with vinegar and spices and baking them. When so treated, they provided a tasty dish eaten cold and could be stored for weeks.

Foreign fishermen came to Cornwall too. Well into the 1930s, in fact right up to the outbreak of war in 1939, Breton fishermen sailed their crabbers to Cornish waters, and took crabs, crayfish and lobsters back to France. A sailing crabber, the *Lutin*, fitted with brine tanks to keep the crabs alive, was a regular visitor to Newlyn before the war. The firm of Harvey & Sons, which now has large modern premises for the treatment of shellfish, started in a small way many years ago by trading with the Bretons.

Deep-sea trawlers
Left: Beam trawler
Below: Stern trawler

Trawlers were very unpopular, as indeed they still are. In the nineteenth century, they were not Cornish boats but came from Brixham and the east coast. They scooped up the fish which swam near the bottom, skate, ray, conger and the smaller flatfish but fishermen complained that they also disturbed the shoals near the surface and took young fish instead of leaving them to grow.

Warnings about the damaging effect of trawlers operating close to land have gone unheeded and in recent years there have been troubles over the use of trawls to catch mackerel of any size. From the present state of fishing around Cornwall it seems that the results of over-fishing have been just as the older fishermen predicted. Unless small fish are left to grow, there will be no fish left for anybody.

'Toshers' – small boats
for inshore fishing
(*below and opposite page*)

Modern trawlers at Newlyn

Newlyn is still an important port and is growing. The main boats are now locally-owned trawlers but there is a small fleet of 'toshers', small open boats which fish inshore with nets or with lines having thousands of hooks. Newlyn harbour is a large one. In one corner is a small horseshoe-shaped pier dating from the fourteenth century. The two outer piers were added in the late nineteenth century and there is a new pier, recently opened by the Queen, which provides more berthing space. There are no seine boats operating regularly but there are one or two left, ready to go out if a large shoal appears.

It may be thought that while fishing was so busy an industry, all the fishermen were well off. This was not the case and few of them made much more than a bare living. When fish were plentiful, prices were low and when prices were high, fish

There were many old sayings about the fish trade. The pilchards coming in at harvest time gave rise to the verse;

> When the corn is in the shock,
> Then the fish are on the rock.

It was also said that: 'A good year for fleas is a good year for fish.' This probably meant that a warm summer bred a lot of fleas and also brought fish in large numbers. Another saying, referring to the great value of fish, said: 'Food, money and light–all in one night.'

Fishermen also said that pilchards should be eaten from the tail to the head or the shoals would be driven away from the shore and that when the fish being pressed made a squeaking sound, caused by their swim-bladders collapsing, they were crying for more of their companions to come to join them.

Fishermen were very superstitious and there were many words which could not be spoken when fishing, for fear of bad luck and a poor catch. It was considered unlucky to mention rabbits or hares, for instance. Women on board were sure to bring trouble and whistling was absolutely forbidden.

The names given to the boats reflected the family nature of the work and the fisherman's simple faith in God and the Bible. *Emily, Our Katie, Two Boys, Jane,* and *Three Brothers* are instances of the first and *Galilean, Nazarene, Twelve Apostles, Guide Me, Ebenezer* and *Star of Bethlehem* are all Bible names and words. There

were hard to find. Good seasons were frequently followed by bad ones and a common saying was 'choked or starved'. Seine boats were mainly owned by companies and the men in them received a wage plus a share of the profits. Other boats were owned by a group of men, often from the same family, and the money earned was shared. The boat itself received a share, which went on its upkeep.

When times were hard, the people in the fishing villages were in poverty and sometimes had to eat limpets and mussels gathered from the rocks at low tide. They called it 'tryg-meat', an interesting example of how Cornish words survived, because 'tryg' means low tide in Cornish. Another dish used by the poor was a thin, watery gruel called 'sky-blue and sinker'. When boats installed engines, they had a small winch on deck to help haul in the nets or lines. It was always known as a 'jinny', another word in the Cornish language. Cornish for machine is 'jyn'.

are more Cornish names now than there were a few years ago. At Newlyn, there are, *Tyak an Mor* = Farmer of the Sea, *Morvoren* = Mermaid, and the Cornwall Sea Fisheries launch kept there is the *Palores* = Chough.

Cornish fishermen have occasionally made history. In May, 1896, there was a serious event at Newlyn which caused troops to be sent there to keep the peace. It has passed into Cornwall's history as The Newlyn Riots. It was not the custom for Cornish fishermen to go to sea on Sundays. This was the Sabbath, a day of rest and a day for going to church and chapel. Visiting east coast fishermen, however, had no such respect for the day and went fishing as usual. This meant that they were able to land catches on Monday morning when prices were high.

There had always been arguments about this between the two sets of fishermen and, in 1896, they broke out into open fighting. Returning east coast boats had their fish dumped overboard or found Newlyn harbour barred to them. Extra police were sent to the village and a detachment of soldiers came down by train from Plymouth. After a few days, peace was restored but several Newlyn men were tried in court at Bodmin for their part. Fines were imposed but nobody was sent to prison although this had been expected.

In 1937, a Newlyn boat, the *Rosebud*, sailed to London and moored close by the Houses of Parliament. Those on board carried a petition to the government, asking that a new housing scheme in the village should not be carried out. Fishermen complained that the new houses were too far from their work and that their existing homes would be destroyed without good reason.

The petition did not succeed but the voyage caused great interest throughout the whole country. The empty cottages were still intact when war came in 1939 and in 1940 they were taken over by Belgian fishermen and their families who had fled from their own country when it was captured by the Germans. For the next four years, the Belgians carried on their lives in Cornwall, with their own school and church, their own customs and their own way of life.

Longer ago, a small sailing lugger, the *Mystery*, made an epic voyage from Newlyn to Australia. This is described more fully in a later chapter.

One of the Newlyn fishwives in 1851, Mary Kelynack, caused a small sensation when she walked to London to see the Great Exhibition there. She was eighty-five years old. Dressed in the traditional way, she put her few belongings into her fish cowel and refused all offers of lifts in carts and coaches. Her arrival attracted much friendly attention and she was introduced to the Lord Mayor and to Queen Victoria. She returned home by train and coach and lived until the age of eighty-eight. In Newlyn, there is a plaque showing the site of the cottage where she once lived.

In wartime, many fishermen have gone to join the Royal Navy or have stayed at home in the patrol service, using their fishing boats, painted grey, to spot mines and submarines and to check on merchant ships and their cargoes.

An unpaid job for scores of Cornish fishermen has been to man the lifeboats stationed around the coast. In this dangerous work they have shown great skill and bravery and saved thousands of lives. Sometimes, they have given their own, as at St Ives in 1938, when the lifeboat capsized, and at Penlee in 1981, when the whole crew of eight was lost while trying to rescue the crew of the *Union Star*.

To be a fisherman is to know the ways of the wind and the sea as well as the ways of the fish beneath the waves. The ocean is not a friendly place, however beautiful it looks in the summer when the sun sparkles on it. Fishermen use it, but they respect it. The ancient Bible writer knew what he was talking about when he said,

These men see the works of the Almighty, and His wonders in the deep.

Some Things To Do

1 Go to one of our fishing harbours and look for old fish cellars.

2 Look at the boats and try to discover how they fish. Is it with nets, lines, trawls or crab pots? Try to find out the purpose of the pieces of equipment used.

3 Try to find out what happens to the fish caught. Where does it go, and how does it travel?

4 Look at the boats and find out where they come from. Each has a registration mark. For instance, PZ = Penzance.

5 Make a list of boats' names. Is there any pattern in their choice?

6 If you live near Newlyn and can get up very early go to the market to see the fish landed and sold.

A plaque to Mary Kelynack, a Newlyn fishwife

Chapter 7

CORNWALL'S CHURCHES AND CHAPELS

The Celtic monks did most of their preaching in the open air. When they did build churches, they were simple buildings of stones, wood and thatch. Saxon builders added very little as their rule in Cornwall only lasted a hundred years or so.

There are some very old Celtic and Saxon fonts in our present churches but the only building dating from this period is the tiny oratory, or chapel, of St Piran at Perranzabuloe. This is now re-buried beneath the sands but is of uncemented stone, about eight metres long and four wide.

In 1066, the Normans invaded England and after the Battle of Hastings they became masters of all the island. With William the Conqueror and later kings, the country was unified under one ruler. Not even distant Cornwall escaped the new laws and the new ways. Those who had helped William in his conquest were given rewards and one, Robert of Mortain, was given the whole of Cornwall as his own. He took the title of Earl of Cornwall, a name used by his successors also. They were the people who built the castles we see today at Trematon, near Saltash; Tintagel, Restormel and Launceston.

Once they were secure in their rule, they built many churches, and although much of what they made has been destroyed by later builders, enough remains to show us what their work was like. Just as the Celtic saints built their little churches on the sites of pagan meeting-places, so the Normans often built their new churches where the Celtic oratories stood. When the new builders pulled these down, to make way for larger and more splendid buildings, they used the stones for their own work. Sometimes, they kept parts of the old buildings intact and simply built on to them. So when we look at our Cornish churches, we do not often find a structure which was built by one set of masons. Usually, it has examples of the work and styles of many centuries.

Norman stonemasons were skilled in their craft and, in their original land of Normandy, they had already built many fine castles and monasteries. In Cornwall, there was an inexhaustable supply of good stone but Norman masons often found that it was too hard for the best use of their tools. Some stone was brought across the sea from Normandy and they selected the best of local material, choosing it not only for its texture but for its colour. Their favourite Cornish quarries were at Polyphant, not far from Launceston, and at Cataclewse, near Padstow. Near the Lizard, they made good use of serpentine stone, which can be polished to look like marble.

Although they were good builders, they had not discovered how to make slender pillars or thin, high walls to support a great weight of masonry. All their churches had very thick walls and massive columns, to support round-headed arches. Norman churches resemble castles. Both kinds of buildings were built by the same masons, using the same techniques.

There is Norman work in more than one hundred and thirty Cornish churches that is easily identified. Some of the most spectacular can be seen in the church at St German's, near Saltash,

The west front of the great church at St. German's. The two towers are of different shapes because the one on the left was finished long after the other, by which time fashion had changed.

Left: The Norman doorway at St. German's

Norman windows

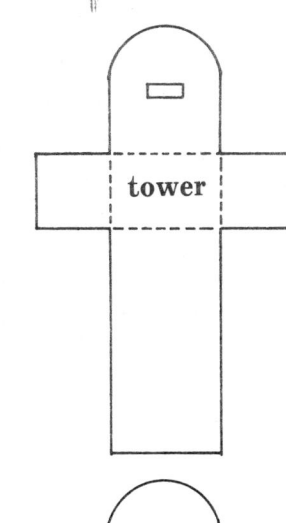

The plan of many Norman churches.

Cruciform or cross-shaped

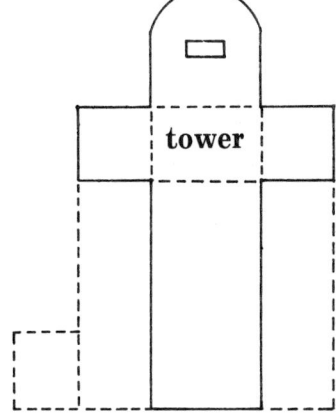

Later the churches were often enlarged by building at the sides

where St Germanus established a monastery in the fifth century. Here lived the first Cornish bishops, until the rule of the church in our land was transferred to Exeter. The Norman front has a huge doorway with a round arch and the windows are built to the same pattern. The decoration is a zig-zag, or chevron, carving. This is a feature of all Norman architecture. The finer kinds of stone carving had not then been developed. At St German's, parts of the church were built by later generations, but it is the best and most complete example of their work in Cornwall.

At Kilkhampton, near Bude, there is another great Norman doorway and more of their work can be seen at Morwenstow. At Tintagel, the small church on the clifftop is almost exactly the same as when it was constructed between 1080 and 1150 and it is well worth a visit.

It gives a splendid idea of what the Norman Earls of Cornwall saw and used all those centuries ago. It is built in the shape of a cross, like so many churches of the time, and because of the small windows and heavy masonry it is very dark inside. A Norman arch separates the chancel from the nave and the chevron decorations are everywhere. The dedication is to St Materiana, a Welsh lady who is believed to have brought Christianity to the area about A.D. 500. It is also thought that the Normans built on the site of an earlier Celtic oratory and a later Saxon building. If this is so, then Christian worship has been offered here for at least fourteen hundred years.

In the far west, there is Norman work in the churches at Lelant, and at Landewednack near the Lizard, but there is usually some reference to the Normans in the guidebooks in almost every old Cornish church.

In the fifteenth century, there was another great time of church building. In many places, the existing church had become too small for the number of worshippers, so enlargements were made. A common practice was to add side aisles to one or both sides of the nave. When this was done, the original cross shape was, of course, lost. By this time, masons had learned new skills and knew how to make arches tall and pointed, and the walls less thick. The new buildings were much more graceful and less dark. Study of the architecture shows how the openings for doors, arches and windows progressed from the thick walls and round-headed arches of the Normans, through the low pointed arches of the later masons to the high graceful openings and soaring roofs of the fifteenth and sixteenth centuries. Towers were added and stone decoration became much more varied and highly skilled. Windows were filled with stained-glass showing pictures of stories in the Bible. When so few people could read, such illustrations were valuable in bringing the stories to life. Walls were painted in designs of red, blue and green and the timber ceilings were decorated with stars and angels.

A fourteenth-century window in the ruined chapel of St. Thomas a Becket, Bodmin. The skilled mediaeval stonemason could make tall pointed windows and arches.

The mediaeval stonework at Poughill church

We are used to seeing churches with plain stone walls inside, with unpainted furniture, and roofs with exposed timbers. It is necessary to use some imagination to understand that once, those walls were painted plaster, those roofs had plaster ceilings and that there were no seats. On Bodmin Moor, in Blisland church, there are painted and gilded decorations in the ancient style. They seem rather gaudy now but in past centuries all churches were brightly coloured and a good deal of money was lavished on them.

Not only has the internal appearance of our churches altered during the centuries, but the use of the buildings has also changed. At one time, they were used for meetings and local festivities as well as for services. They combined the functions of religious building and church hall. To separate the most sacred part, near the altar at the east end, from the more public sections, it was usual to build a carved wooden screen across the nave. Many of these were elaborately and skilfully carved by dedicated craftsmen. When services became more involved, with more ceremony and with music, seats or benches were added. Bench ends were also decorated with carvings of birds, beasts, stories from the Bible, and even local legends. At Zennor, near Land's End, a most famous carving on the end of a bench shows The Mermaid of Zennor, complete with her fish tail and her looking-glass. Legend says that she visited the church on a number of occasions and sang so beautifully that one young man in the choir followed her to sea and was never seen again.

The rood screen, Blisland church

Carved bench ends, Poughill church

There are a number of carved screens and bench ends still to be seen. Some of the best are at Kilkhampton and Launcells in the north-east of Cornwall but it is always interesting to explore. The smallest and most remote churches often provide the most unusual examples.

The rood screen in Bodmin Parish Church. Although not the original it contains woodwork from the fifteenth century and gives an idea of what a beautifully carved screen was like.

In the fifteenth and sixteenth centuries, when some of our most beautiful parish churches were built, the chief service was the Mass, or Holy Communion, which was conducted with great ceremony and an air of mystery.

The screen added to the mystery as the people standing outside could not easily see the priest at the altar. At one point in the service came a reading from the Bible, delivered by the priest from the top of the screen. He and his assistants stood by the carving of Christ which occupied the centre. The statues there were called the 'rood' and the correct name of the screen is the 'rood screen'. There were stairs in the walls leading to the top of the screen and these can still be seen in scores of churches, even though the screen may have gone. If you find a small door and a set of stairs leading to an opening high in the wall you will know that there was once a rood screen at that spot. At St Levan, near the Lizard, there are three sets of stairs, probably the result of alterations over many years.

In some places, you will find a square hole cut through the wall separating a side chapel from the main altar. These are called squints and they enabled a worshipper standing in the side chapel to see the priest at the altar.

In the sixteenth century, there was much argument about religion and how services ought to be conducted. The head of the Christian church was the Pope in Rome and there were no divisions into Roman Catholics, Church of England, Methodists or other groups. There was only one Church and only one way of worship. The arguments are difficult to understand but, in the most simple terms, they were between those who wanted to continue in the old ways, with much ceremony and mystery, and those who wished to simplify the services and to make them more understandable to ordinary people.

A German monk, Martin Luther, was the leader of those who 'protested' against what they saw as the wickedness of the Church. His followers became known as Protestants. Those who followed tradition became known as Catholics, or Roman Catholics. In England, in the sixteenth century, King Henry VIII, quarrelled with the Pope. He said that as King of England he was also Head of the Church of England.

Thus began a quarrel which rages to this day. In Britain the form of worship remained much the same for a long time but those priests and people who saw the Pope as the religious leader were henceforth regarded as possible traitors to the country and they often suffered for it. Those who wished to do away with statues, candles, incense and all the outward show in religion were encouraged to try even harder to make sweeping changes.

The religious arguments were mixed up with political ones and in the seventeenth century, the two sets of supporters came to open warfare. In 1642, King Charles I and his royalists began a long struggle against Parliament and its army. Their differences were very great and, although religion was not a main reason for going to war, the King's party generally supported the old ways, while those who were on the side of Parliament were all for getting rid of anything to do with the Pope and his priests. The most ardent of them were nick-named Puritans because of their wish to live in a simple, 'pure', manner.

The Civil War lasted for seven years and battles were fought up and down the land. Cornwall, as a whole, supported the King and supported him so well that he wrote a letter of thanks to the people of Cornwall for all they had done for him. There are several Cornish churches which have part of this letter painted on the walls, surmounted by the badge of Charles I.

At first, the King's armies did well. A Parliamentary army which invaded Cornwall was defeated and thrown back over the Tamar but, as the years went on, the forces of Parliament gained the upper hand. Their soldiers, known as Roundheads because of their short hair, invaded Cornwall again and many towns were occupied by them. At Lostwithiel, they used the church as a stable and, to show their contempt for the old religion, they smashed hundreds of beautiful stained glass windows, destroyed carvings and paintings and took away gold and silver objects to be sold for money to continue the war.

Most of the stained-glass in our Cornish churches today is not very old but at St Neot, in east Cornwall, there are some of the finest examples in the British Isles. For some reason, the windows there escaped destruction by the Roundheads and they are almost as they were two hundred years before the Civil War.

There are many signs of the damage caused by the Parliamentary troops. Missing rood screens may have been taken down by them and burned in the churchyard or in their barracks, angels with missing heads may have had them struck off by a sword or a musket butt, and there is the occasional bullet hole to be seen in a church door or a pulpit. Perhaps the most telling signs are on the lists of vicars posted on the church walls. If you examine them for the years between 1645 and 1660 you will frequently find no name recorded because the priest then in charge was removed by Parliament for being a King's man.

When the Civil War was over, there was a period of eleven years without either king or queen. England was ruled by a military government and harsh punishments were given to many who had supported Charles I. Heavy fines were imposed on some Cornish landowners. Great houses fell into disrepair, fields were left untended and it was an unhappy time for all. Nothing was ever the same again, not even when King Charles II was invited to return to rule over his country in 1660.

There were now two religions in the land, Protestant and Catholic, and a large number of Dissenters, people who did not believe in the ways of either. The most important group of Dissenters in Cornwall was the Quakers, a peace-loving religious organization founded by George Fox, who was born in Leicestershire in 1624. The Quakers met in private houses or in small meeting-houses, had no paid ministers and no set form of religious service. George Fox travelled widely and was once imprisoned for several months in the Doomsdale Tower of Launceston Castle. He and several friends were arrested in St Ives for handing out religious papers. Taken to Launceston, they refused to pay the fines and were thus shut up in the ruins of the old castle. A plaque on the wall of the castle records the event.

The title 'Quakers' is a nick-name. The correct name is The Society of Friends. They tended to keep themselves apart from others, probably because they were often jeered at and derided. On the road from Penzance to Land's End, only a short distance from the village of Sennen Churchtown, is a tiny walled churchyard. It stands deserted by the roadside and is now in ruin, with the grass high over the gravestones. It is a Quaker cemetery and at one time was a well-known local landmark, respected as the Friends' Burial Ground.

A carved panel in Madron church showing the badge of Henry VII and the Tudor rose.
It is believed to have been installed by Parson Tregos, vicar from 1498 to 1534. He had supported Perkin Warbeck during his attempt to gain the throne in 1497 and had been charged with high treason, but was pardoned on payment of a heavy fine. Perhaps this was an attempt to prove his loyalty to Henry VII.

Cornwall's parish churches tell the story of our villages and towns through the centuries. They are similar in that all have altars and seats, towers and churchyards, but they are all unique in that each one says something special about its own community and its own part in Cornwall's history. In many areas of Great Britain, you will see lofty churches with soaring spires and great treasures and tombs within. In Cornwall, churches are usually quite small and ruggedly built to withstand the gales and storms which sweep across our small land. There are very few spires and their Celtic origins can be seen in their dedications, three-quarters of which are to Celtic saints. In the churchyards, there are numerous Celtic crosses, and many modern ones are in the Celtic shape. The memorials inside tell the stories of men and woman who helped shape Cornwall's history and occasionally, though not often, there are fragments of the old Cornish language to be seen.

The memorials to those who have long since died would take a book to themselves to describe properly. Here are a few of the most interesting ones. In Pelynt church, near Looe, there are monuments to the famous Cornish family of Trelawny. One of them was a lawyer, Edward Trelawny, who died in 1630. His inscription was obviously written by someone who did not have a high opinion of the honesty of lawyers at that time.

This is what he said:

> Here lies an honest lawyer, wot ye what;
> A thing for all the world to wonder at.

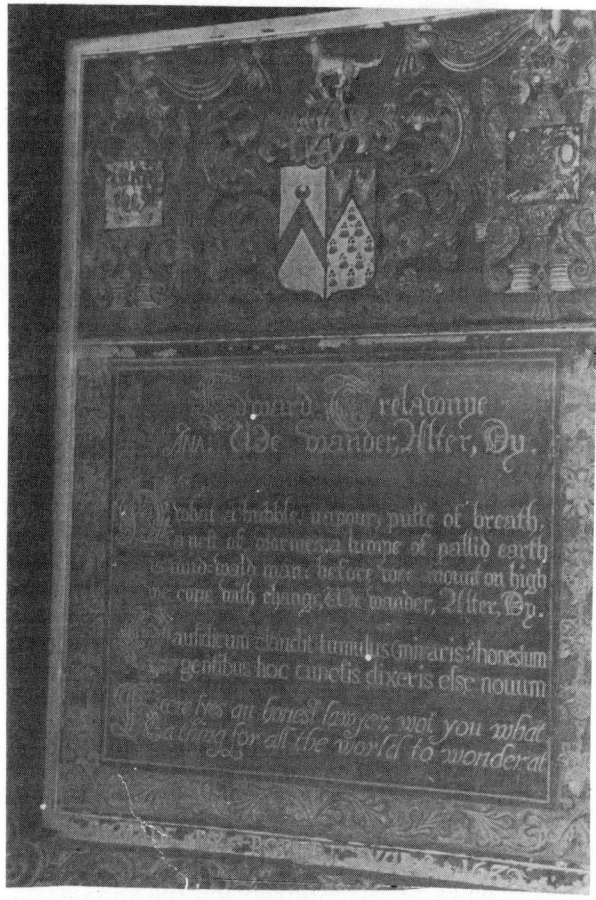

The tomb of Edward Trelawny, 1630

Another, marvelling at the honesty of not one, but two, lawyers is at St Buryan:

> Here lie John and Richard Benn,
> Two lawyers and two honest men.
> God works miracles now and then.

At Lansallos, near Polperro, there is a tombstone by the church door to the memory of a young sailor, 'accidentally killed by a Cannonball fired by a person unknown'. Perhaps he was a smuggler killed by the revenue men while running a cargo of brandy into the bay. Joseph Grapp, buried at Mylor in 1770, also came to an unfortunate end:

> His foot, it slip and he did fall,
> Help, Help, he cried, and that was all.

Writers of these old inscriptions were fond of playing games with words. At Mevagissey, there is a slate memorial to a Tudor family called Dart. Father is shown with his six sons and Mother with her two daughters, all dressed in their best Elizabethan clothes. The epitaph enjoys the various meanings of the word Dart:

> Death shoots sometimes as archers do,
> One dart to find another;
> But now by shooting hath found four
> And all laid here together.

In Bodmin church is a slate tombstone showing the entire Durant family, Richard Durant, once mayor of the town, with two wives and twenty children. The inscription: MODERATA DURANT (meaning, roughly, Moderation Lasts) is a pun on his name and makes a joke of the fact that he had so many children.

When you visit Cornish churches you never know what you are likely to find. Perhaps the work of the Normans, perhaps a fine tomb to a member of a noble family, perhaps a simpler monument to a famous engineer, soldier, sailor or benefactor. If there are none of these, you will certainly see memorials to more simple people who lived in and around the church, and the church itself is a memorial to all the Cornish people who have ever had anything to do with it.

A Tudor tomb in Pelynt church showing Mother, Father and all the children

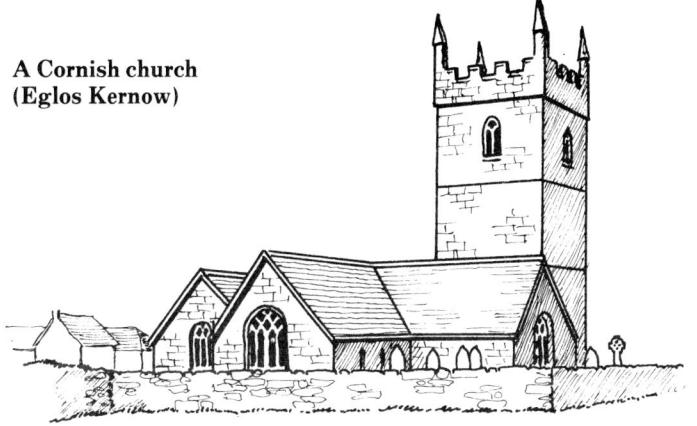

A Cornish church
(Eglos Kernow)

An early Methodist chapel

Some of the later Methodist churches
were large and splendid buildings

Parish churches are not the only religious buildings in Cornwall and we must not forget the scores of simple wayside chapels which tell the story of the great crusade of Methodism which swept the whole country in the eighteenth century. In Cornwall, it had a great and lasting effect, especially in the far west.

In 1743, a man called John Wesley visited Cornwall for the first time, with his brother Charles. They were both clergymen of the Church of England but were very different from some of the parish clergy of the time. Far too many of these were the sons of rich families who had become parsons because it seemed to offer the easy life of a country gentleman. They lived in large and splendid houses, kept many servants and spent a good deal of their time in hunting and other social pursuits. Such men allowed the life of their parishes to fall into bad ways and they did nothing to combat the poverty, crime and squalor which were very common. The rich were rich and the poor were poor, and it was God's will that it should be so, according to the thinking of many powerful men in government and in the Church. The rich country parson had more sympathy with the ways of the rich than with the troubles of the poor.

The Wesleys and their friends were against this attitude and wanted the Church to return to the more down-to-earth teachings of the Bible, a religion without show or ceremony, where the priest lived and worked with his flock. When they were young men at the University in Oxford, they formed a club for those who believed in their ideas. The rules called for a strict discipline and because they lived so methodically they became known as Methodists.

John and Charles Wesley rode all over the country, preaching the lessons of Christ and trying to show people a new kind of life based on the Bible. They slept where they could, in the open air, in barns and in cottages if the owners would take them in. They preached in town and village squares, on beaches and on grassy banks, wherever there were people to listen to them.

Only rarely did they preach in church, for clergymen generally were against them. They were thought to be dangerous agitators, putting revolutionary ideas into the heads of simple people. Bishops spoke out against them and local

magistrates tried to prevent them from speaking. Those who listened and supported them often found themselves in trouble from employers or landlords.

When they first came to Cornwall, very few folk listened with sympathy. They were thought to be cranks, so were targets for stones, mud and abuse. Slowly, their message began to be received and they gained support, sometimes from those who had been first among the stone-throwers. Just as the first apostles of Christ organized little groups of Christians in towns and cities which they visited, so the Wesleys organized groups of Methodists. They appointed leaders and left them to carry on the work for them, in houses, barns and lofts and in the open air. Sometimes, the groups split up because of quarrels and difficulties. Sometimes, they grew in numbers and strength.

John Wesley came to Cornwall forty times. Each time, he found that Methodism was stronger and that people were beginning to respect what he had to say. Methodism became a new way of life for thousands. Scores of men gave up wicked ways and became model citizens. There is no doubt that they did a tremendous amount of good and gave poor, ordinary men and women a feeling that they

51

too were important in life. Methodism never became popular with the Church. One of John Wesley's few friends among the clergy, the Vicar of St Gennys, was threatened by the Bishop that if he continued to have anything to do him, he would make him resign.

Wesley was a very energetic man. He rode thousands of miles on his horse, or walked, and it must be remembered that there were then few good roads in Cornwall. Most were rutted and pot-holed tracks, full of dust in summer and water in winter. He often travelled thirty miles and preached four or five times in a single day. He relied on charity for food and his companions worked at odd jobs to earn a few coins.

But, as we have said, as the years went on his power grew and the love of the people grew stronger. In the end, Mr Wesley, as he was known, was probably the most famous man in Cornwall. To have spoken to Mr Wesley personally was considered to be a great honour.

He was a short man and, when he preached, he always looked for a high spot on which to stand. Some of the rocks on which he stood became objects of reverence in Cornwall. At Heamoor, just outside Penzance, a rock on which he preached now forms the base of the pulpit in the Methodist Chapel, built in 1842 and called Wesley Rock Chapel. At Trewint, on the A30 road across Bodmin Moor, there is a tiny cottage kept as a memorial to him. In it once lived Digory and Elizabeth Isbell, two of his first and most faithful followers. In Wesley's Journals, the diaries in which he recorded his work, there are many references to them and to 'the house with the stone porch' where he frequently stayed.

The Isbells illustrate the fact, often forgotten, that Wesley was always a member of the Church of England and had no wish to form a separate organization. They were regular attenders at Altarnun Church and are buried in the churchyard there, but they also promoted the Methodist cause. There are only two rooms in the cottage and in the upper room are books and pictures about the early days of Methodism and the life of John Wesley.

Digory Isbell's cottage at Altarnun, now a memorial to Wesley

The old chapel, Altarnun. The bust of John Wesley over the door is by Neville Northey Burnard.

Left: Altarnun church

The greatest Methodist preaching-place in Cornwall is Gwennap Pit, near Redruth. This is a large and deep hollow, formed by the collapse of underground mine-workings. One day, wishing to preach to a large crowd, and being troubled by a high wind which blew his words away, Wesley went into the pit for shelter. He found that his preaching could be heard clearly by everybody and so it became a regular site for his work. In later years, local Methodists cut ledges into the banks inside, providing seating for thousands. An annual service is still held there in his memory.

The Church of England allowed only clergymen to preach. John Wesley encouraged ordinary men to do so. Such men were called 'local preachers' and they travelled from place to place in all weathers to conduct services on Sundays and on weekdays. One of the most famous was a miner called Billy Bray, who lived near Gwennap with his wife and five children. Poorly educated, he was enormously enthusiastic and, like all the early Methodists, had a wonderful knowledge of the Bible.

Every day, Billy Bray worked in the mines and in his spare time he laboured for Methodism. He built three chapels by himself and helped with the building of many others. In addition, he preached every Sunday, walking great distances to carry out his duties. He did it all for the love of God. This is what he wrote about his work:

I was a very poor man with a wife and five small children, and I worked in the mine underground. Sometimes, I was forenoon core (that is, working in the morning), and when I had taken my dinner I would go to the Chapel and work as long as I could see, and the next day do the same. The next week I should be afternoon core, and then I would go up to the Chapel in the morning and work until midday, and then go home and away to the mine. The week following, I would be night core. I would then work about the Chapel by day and go to mine at night, and had not the dear Lord greatly strengthened me for the work, I could not have done it. When I was about the Chapel, I also had potatoes to teel (plant) in my garden, and every Sunday I was planned to preach. Some Sundays I had to walk twenty miles and speak three times. I have worked twenty hours in the twenty-four, and had not the Lord helped me I could not have done it.

We can only marvel at his enormous energy and devotion and wonder how he could possibly have fitted in so much work in each day and night.

The work of building chapels in which to hold services was a natural result of the growth of Methodism. Methodists were denied a place in the existing parish churches so, as their numbers grew, they decided to build their own. As they were not rich, they could not afford anything splendid. They gave what they had most of, their skills and their time. Like Billy Bray, they worked after or before work to erect simple chapels, some of stone but many of cob, a mixture of clay, chopped straw and lime, with thatched roofs. When finished, they were white-washed inside and out. There were no candles, except to give light, no ornaments and no religious pictures or statues. As their worship was based on the Bible, there were plenty of seats, grouped around the most important point, the pulpit.

Singing was also important in their services, for they liked to praise God with cheerful songs and the Wesley brothers wrote many fine hymns. Choirs were popular and as there were originally no organs or pianos, the singing was led by somebody with a good voice. He could be relied on to start everybody off on the right note, so was called the 'pitcher'.

In more modern times, some splendid and large chapels were built of dressed granite and in the best architectural style. In Cornwall, Methodism was very strong in the poorest and most hard-working communities, the fishing villages and the mining villages. It is here that one finds the very big chapels, in Camborne and St Just, for instance. At one time, they were full every Sunday and the singing in them was something never to be forgotten. There was great rivalry between 'church people' and 'chapel people', something which Wesley never intended, and sometimes, it must be said, the two sets of worshippers actively hated each other and put obstacles in each other's way.

A small wayside Methodist chapel at Newbridge. It is typical of hundreds built in the nineteenth century.

A large and splendid Wesleyan church in Bodmin. Many, like this one, had large Sunday and Day schools attached.

Some Things To Do

1 Find out something of the history of your parish church. To which saint is it dedicated?

2 Try to identify the workmanship of the different periods of building. Look for the rood loft stairs. Is there a really old Screen?

3 Read the memorial tablets on the walls and look at the old tombstones in the churchyard to find out some of the history of the parish.

4 Look at the list of Vicars. What happened in the Civil War years?

5 How old is the local Methodist chapel? They often have a date inscribed on them.

6 Visit the chapel and the church for a service and see the differences in the way of worship.

7 Read a book called *What to look for in Cornish Churches*, visit some taking the book with you.

8 Visit Gwennap Pit to see where John Wesley preached, and Wesley Cottage at Trewint on Bodmin Moor.

9 Make a point of never leaving a Cornish village without looking inside the church. You will have some surprises.

John Wesley died in 1791, having founded a way of worship which has spread all over the world. In Cornwall, it is still a powerful force but the chapels are no longer filled as they once were. Neither, of course, are the churches. The way of life has changed, and there are many who would say that it has not changed for the better. Scores of the tiny wayside chapels have been turned into barns or houses. Some have been destroyed to make way for other buildings. Some, like the thatched one at the foot of Roseworthy Hill between Hayle and Camborne in which Billy Bray preached many times, have simply fallen down.

Times change and we change with them. Our churches and chapels stand as living reminders of the faith of our forefathers, even though they may no longer be the vital force they once were. With all our modern skills and inventions, we cannot truthfully say or believe that we are any wiser, or better people in our lives, than those who built them and who have gone before us.

54

Chapter 8

SOME FAMOUS CORNISHMEN

Cornwall is nearly an island and all its people live by the sea or very close to it. For hundreds of years, the eldest son of the King or Queen of England has been Duke of Cornwall and has had a special claim on the loyalty of Cornish men and women. It is not surprising therefore that during Cornwall's long history, there have been many Cornishmen who have done brave deeds at sea or have fought bravely for the Crown on land.

The most famous name associated with Cornwall is that of King Arthur, who lived about fifteen hundred years ago. Everybody has heard of him and the stories of the Knights of the Round Table. Thousands of visitors come to Tintagel every year to see what they suppose to be his castle on the clifftop and the cave of Merlin the Magician on the beach below. It is all very romantic and exciting but the truth is that the stories are all imaginary. Arthur is claimed as a special hero throughout south-west Britain, in Wales and even in Scotland. We can only guess at the truth from the few bits of writing which have come down to us.

When the English tribes were conquering more and more of Britain and the Celts were being forced farther and farther into the west, there *was* a great Celtic leader called Arthur. He must have been a great man, skilled and brave in battle and able to unite the different tribes in their struggles against the invaders. As the fighting moved ever westward he probably moved his headquarters many times and so became well known throughout the whole of the south-western peninsula. When he was killed, the Celts lost their greatest leader.

According to Cornish legend, he was mortally wounded at a place just outside Camelford with the grim name of Slaughter Bridge. You will see it marked on the map and by it, a spot known as Arthur's Grave. On Bodmin Moor, there is a place called King Arthur's Hall and legend also says that a large hill fort at Kellybury, near Wadebridge, was his Cornish home. In the far west, near the village of Mousehole there is a rock known as the Merlin, with Merlin's Cave nearby. In the Isles of Scilly, we find two rocks called Great and Little Arthur and one legend says that he was buried in these islands. Some say that his royal palace of Camelot took its name from the area around the River Camel in north Cornwall.

We just do not know what the truth is, for there are as many legends about him in other regions of the south-west. The stories about the Knights of the Round Table were invented many years after his death by a man called Geoffrey of Monmouth and other, later, writers. Geoffrey of Monmouth had heard about Arthur and he probably knew the ancient castle on the headland at Tintagel. He decided that it would make a wonderful home for his hero so he wove his stories around it. In all the exciting tales, Arthur and his Knights are placed in a time about six hundred years after he had really lived. People liked the stories of heroism and good deeds so much that they came to believe that they were really true and the village of Tintagel has become popular and prosperous because of them.

King Arthur now represents the Celtic spirit of Cornwall. He reminds all Cornish people of their Celtic past, their history and their language. On the Cornish badge, you will often see the picture of a bird called a chough. It is a large black bird with a red bill and red legs, a member of the crow family. At one time it was common but, in Cornwall, now exists only in captivity in zoos or bird sanctuaries. It reminds us of yet another legend about King Arthur. A story says that one day Arthur will return to restore Cornwall to Celtic independence and that he still lives, in the disguise of a chough. Sometimes, on pictures of the chough, you will see these Cornish words written: 'Nyns yu marow Myghtern Arthur'. They mean, 'King Arthur is not dead'. The Celtic spirit lives on.

Thomas Flamank and
Michael Joseph (An Gof)

Although neither of these two men was a soldier, together they led a serious rebellion against King Henry VII in 1497. The new king had seized the throne from Richard III in 1485 and now demanded new taxes to pay for a war against Scotland. In Cornwall there was already great poverty, especially among the tin-workers, and Scotland was so far away that England's war there meant nothing to them. There was great anger among the people and many refused to pay the King's Commissioners when they came collecting.

At St Keverne, near the Lizard, the local black-smith, Michael Joseph, roused the men to open rebellion and in Bodmin a lawyer named Thomas Flamank also urged people to take arms and march on London to protest. So, in the summer of 1497, an ill-armed and ill-clad army marched across the Tamar, collecting supporters all the way. In Somerset they were joined by Lord Audley who took general command of the so-called army. When they reached Blackheath on the outskirts of the capital they numbered several thousands, armed with staves, pitchforks, knives and assorted home-made weapons. Here, things began to go wrong. The men of Kent refused to join them, knowing that the King had an army of ten thousand in the city and when this became generally known many others took fright and deserted.

On 17 June, 1497, they were surrounded by the King's army and although the Cornishmen fought bravely under the leadership of Flamank and Michael Joseph they were soon defeated and about two hundred were killed. Lord Audley and Flamank were captured on the battlefield and Joseph was taken as he fled towards Greenwich. When Henry VII rode through London after the battle, the blacksmith was led captive behind him before being shut up in the Tower with the other leaders. It is said that he bore himself bravely and wore a jacket in the King's colours of green and white.

Ten days later, Flamank and Joseph were executed at Tyburn and Lord Audley was beheaded at Tower Hill on the following day. Thus ended the Cornish revolt. But the defeat only fanned the flames of discontent in Cornwall and encouraged a claimant to the throne, Perkin Warbeck, to land in Cornwall in the September of 1497, in the hope of raising another army for a march on London. He claimed to be a brother of Edward V and was received with enthusiasm in Cornwall, being proclaimed King Richard IV at Bodmin. Once again the Cornishmen marched across the Tamar and laid siege to Exeter. The story of that fight and their defeat is told in another chapter.

At his execution Michael Joseph is said to have boasted that he would have 'a name perpetual and a fame permanent and immortal' but he was largely forgotten until 1966 when a memorial to him and Flamank was erected in St Keverne. He is now usually known as An Gof, the Cornish for 'the smith'. The Flamank family remained important in Bodmin and the name is remembered there by a housing estate called Flamank Park.

It may be said that these two men were rebels against the lawful Government and that they cruelly misled the Cornishmen who followed them. It can also be said that they were the leaders in a just fight against oppression and became martyrs in a noble cause. Whatever the case, their revolt shows that the people of Cornwall at this time still considered themselves to be an independent people, loyal enough to the King of England but unwilling to accept what they saw as harsh treatment by the English rulers.

The Grenvilles

By the time of the Norman Conquest in 1066, Cornwall had lost its independence, although all Cornish people still spoke their native Celtic language and thought of themselves as belonging to a separate nation. By the time of Henry VIII, in the sixteenth century, most Cornish men and women knew English, and in the east spoke it as their main language. Some Cornish men had become rich and powerful in the service of the King and, so, gladly gave him their loyalty and help in time of war.

One of the most famous of the powerful Cornish families was the Grenvilles, who lived in a great house at Stowe, in North Cornwall near Kilkhampton, and they became heroes on land and sea.

In 1545, Roger Grenville was the captain of the *Mary Rose*, one of King Henry's most splendid warships. England was at war with France and the *Mary Rose*, laden with soldiers, sailors and all the weapons of war, sailed from The Solent to join the fleet. Within sight of the shore, she was caught by a sudden squall, capsized and sunk, taking with her about five hundred men including her captain. The exciting thing about this wreck is that in 1982 the *Mary Rose* was raised from the seabed and brought to the shore, where she provides an enormous amount of information about ships of Tudor times. Many of the weapons, tools and odds and ends of Tudor life have been carefully cleaned and, along with the surviving parts of the ship, are now on permanent display.

Sir Richard Grenville

Roger Grenville left a son, a little boy of three called Richard. He later became one of our greatest heroes, Grenville of the *Revenge*. He was a cousin of Sir Walter Raleigh and a friend of Sir Francis Drake. In 1585, he commanded a fleet of five ships carrying colonists to the new land of Virginia and on the way home captured a much larger Spanish ship in a fierce fight. In 1591, while second-in-command to Lord Thomas Howard he took a fleet of six warships, six store-ships and several smaller craft to the Azores Islands in the Atlantic, to lie in wait for a Spanish fleet laden with treasure from the Americas.

His own ship was the *Revenge*, which had been Drake's ship in the great fight against the Spanish Armada. While the English fleet lay at anchor in the Azores, with many of the sailors sick ashore, the Spaniards heard about their plan and sent a great fleet of their own to protect their treasure ships. Lord Howard decided that he was not strong enough to fight against them so he gave orders for them to take their sick men on board, raise the anchors and put to sea.

Richard Grenville refused to leave his ninety sick men and said he would stay and fight, no matter how strong his enemy. At about three o'clock in the afternoon on 31 August, 1591, a terrible battle began. Grenville in the *Revenge*, with about a hundred men, fought against fifty Spanish ships with about five thousand men in them. The battle raged fiercely until darkness fell, the cannon balls flying murderously through the air and the smoke covering friend and foe alike. When dawn came the next day, the Spaniards were amazed to see that the *Revenge* still floated, without masts or sails, with the holds flooded, with only twenty men still left to fight, wounded, but still ready for the final battle. Grenville himself lay mortally wounded on the deck but refused to surrender. Calling his chief gunner, he ordered him to sink the ship so that it should not be captured. The few remaining sailors begged him to surrender, saying that further fighting was useless. Hearing their pleas, Grenville agreed, but only on condition that the Spaniards would grant them the full honours of war and return them to England immediately. The Spanish commander, in honour of their gallant fight, agreed, and so the battle ended.

Richard Grenville died of his wounds, a prisoner in a Spanish ship and the *Revenge*, and fourteen Spanish ships, sank shortly afterwards in a great storm.

It was a sea fight which will be remembered for as long as the stories of famous sailors are written.

Sir Bevil Grenville

A grandson of Richard Grenville, the hero of the *Revenge*, he was born in 1596 near Withiel, west of Bodmin. After studying at Oxford he went into Parliament and represented Cornwall several times between 1621 and 1642. These were the years when the quarrels between King and Parliament became more and more bitter. When the Civil War began in 1642, he gave his full support to Charles I and the Royalist cause.

He raised an army in Cornwall and when the Parliamentary soldiers crossed the Tamar, beat them in many battles and threw them out. The Cornish troops fought bravely under his leadership, especially at Braddock Down, near Lostwithiel, and Stratton Hill, near Bude. Here, the Parliamentary soldiers were in a strong position at the top of a steep slope and had beaten off all attacks. At the end of a long day, the Cornishmen, with very little ammunition left, charged once more up the hill and won the battle after a fierce hand-to-hand fight.

After this, he led his men in a victorious march through Devon into Somerset. They were willing to follow him anywhere and his example of courage helped them to overcome many and great difficulties. King Charles's armies were often poorly led but Grenville stood out as a great leader.

In 1643, the Royalists won a great victory at Lansdown Hill just outside Bath but almost in the very moment of success, Bevil Grenville was mortally wounded. His loss was a disaster for the King as many of the Cornish soldiers refused to fight for leaders they did not know and returned home. His body was carried back across the Tamar and was buried in a tomb in Kilkhampton Church. It was said that he was the most beloved man in Cornwall.

The Grenvilles are remembered in the names of many hotels and roads and there are a number of Lansdown Roads to be found in our towns, to remind us of Sir Bevil.

Sir John Arundell

When a man reaches the age of seventy, he is not expected to fight battles but to live peacefully and quitely and to do nothing more exciting than gardening. When Sir John Arundell became Governor of Pendennis Castle at Falmouth in 1643 he probably thought that it would be a quiet command. Although the Civil War was raging, most of the fighting was far away and we have already seen how Bevil Grenville had thrown the Parliamentary soldiers out of Cornwall.

John Arundell was born at the great house of Trerice at Newlyn East and by 1643 had given years of loyal service to several monarchs. He was present at Tilbury in 1588 when Queen Elizabeth reviewed her troops at a time of great danger from Spain. Because of it Arundell was known as 'Old Tilbury'.

As the war went on the Parliamentary army grew stronger and in 1646 the fighting returned to Cornwall. Town after town was captured and, in March, General Fairfax captured St Mawes Castle and laid siege to Pendennis. Calling on Arundell to surrender, he received the famous defiant answer: 'I will here bury myself before I deliver up this castle to such as fight against His Majesty.'

So the siege began. The great gates were locked, the ramparts were manned and guns blazed out against the attackers. Nothing could get in and nobody could get out. Attempts were made to send in supplies of food and ammunition from France but the boats were caught by the warships cruising offshore.

In July, a message was sent to the King that there was little more the defenders could do as they had nothing to eat and little shot for the guns.

The castle held out until 17 August, when Sir John surrendered to Colonel Richard Townsend. It was not an ignoble defeat. For five months, the garrison had held out bravely under the leadership of a gallant old man and had prevented a large number of Parliamentary troops and ships from fighting elsewhere. The defenders were allowed to leave with the full honours of war, weapons loaded, flags flying and drums beating. Twenty-four officers and nine hundred men came through the gate and were made prisoner but unfortunately many died in the following months through illness and disease.

Parliament was so glad at the capture of Pendennis that it made 22 September a day of general thanksgiving. Only Raglan Castle held out longer during a siege, and then only by two days.

It is a pity that there is no memorial at Pendennis to those brave defenders but visitors can still see the battlements, the great gun batteries and Sir John's apartments.

Admiral Edward Boscawen

Most of our famous Cornish soldiers and sailors had nicknames given to them as a mark of respect and affection. Boscawen was known in the Navy as 'Old Dreadnought', a name given when he took command of HMS *Dreadnought* in 1744. It was said of him that he dreaded nothing except disgrace. There is a Boscawen Street in Truro and the navy still has a ship called Dreadnought.

Born at Tregothnan near Falmouth in 1711, at twelve he joined the Royal Navy and was a Captain at twenty-six. Unlike many captains of that period, he treated his men well and was especially careful about their health. He knew that more men died from sickness than through enemy action.

All his life, he was either fighting in England's wars or busy in Parliament. He was M.P. for Truro several times and during the 1745 Rebellion against the King, raised an army of six thousand Cornishman to fight against The Young Pretender, who was trying to seize the throne.

In 1747, he was Commander-in-Chief of all our soldiers and sailors in India and the East Indies.

His last sea victory was won against the French in 1759 and he saved the country from invasion. France had prepared a large invasion fleet in ports along the Channel and had gathered a fleet of warships at Brest to protect it. Another fleet sailed from Toulon to join it. Boscawen received the news of their sailing while he was in Gibraltar. Many of his ships were undergoing repair and were ill-prepared for battle but he took them to sea and met the French warships on the afternoon of 18 August.

In the battle that followed he won such a victory that the invasion plans were cancelled and never revived. He died in 1761 and is buried in the little church of St Michael Penkevil, near Truro.

Samuel Wallis

A little-known but important seaman, he was born at Lanteglos-by-Camelford in 1728. He served under Admiral Boscawen and was his flag-lieutenant, or personal assistant. In 1766, he was given the command of HMS *Dolphin* to explore the Pacific. At that time, it was believed that there was another great continent to the south of South America, a whole new world to discover and exploit. There is, of course, just such a continent, Antarctica, covered in ice and snow and not yet opened-up for the benefit of man, but Wallis was searching for a land like America.

He sailed around the globe in twenty months and found the islands of Tahiti and Easter Island. His report led to Captain Cook's later voyages. Little was known about the Pacific and the maps produced by these early explorers were invaluable. Wallis was an excellent navigator and although he did not achieve the fame of the greatest explorers, played an important part in their voyages.

Captain William Bligh

Sometimes, one event in a man's life becomes the best-known thing about him. William Bligh, who was born in 1754 in the small village of St Tudy, between Bodmin and Camelford, is well-known for his part in the famous mutiny on HMS *Bounty* in 1789. Few people know the real facts about it.

A very popular film, 'Mutiny on the *Bounty*', showed him as a wicked and cruel man who brought troubles on himself. Those who mutinied were shown as poor, ill-treated sailors who were driven to doing a wrong deed. Most people firmly believe this to be the true story but the film-makers altered many of the facts to make a good story even better.

When he was very young, his family moved to Plymouth, where he joined the Royal Navy as a midshipman. A good sailor, he became a respected and efficient officer. In 1772, he went with Captain Cook on his second voyage round the world and showed himself to be a very clever navigator and mapmaker. Like Samuel Wallis before him, he did much useful work in charting unknown seas.

In 1787, the Admiralty chose him to command the *Bounty* on a voyage to the Pacific to collect plants of the breadfruit tree and to make further scientific study of the islands. The Government thought that if the trees could be replanted and grown in the West Indies they would provide cheap food for the plantation workers.

It was a disastrous voyage. The *Bounty* was not a warship but a small converted merchant vessel and was unsuitable. It was too small and in poor condition. The crew was larger than usual, there were scientists aboard and space had to be kept for the large number of plants they expected to carry. Some of the sailors were known trouble-makers and Bligh did not get on well with some of the officers and petty officers.

By the time they reached the Pacific islands there was much unrest aboard and his attempts to keep discipline caused a mutiny. Bligh and those loyal to him were cast adrift in a longboat with little food and water and only the simplest navigational instruments. The mutineers, led by Fletcher Christian, took the ship to Tahiti and left Bligh to his fate. They hoped that the Admiralty would think the ship and all its crew had been lost in a storm.

Bligh was an excellent navigator and a splendid seaman. In spite of the great difficulties, he sailed the small open boat three and a half thousand miles to Timor, and with the loss of only a few men. From there the news of the mutiny was sent to England. It was a remarkable voyage and at that time the longest open-boat voyage known.

The mutineers quarrelled and nine of them took the *Bounty* to sea again, to look for an uninhabited island. They found one at Pitcairn, burned the ship and settled there with native wives. Their fate was unknown until 1808, when an American ship called there by chance and found the only surviving mutineer, John Adams, living with a number of women and children.

In 1790, those who had stayed on Tahiti had an unwelcome surprise. HMS *Pandora* arrived and twelve mutineers were arrested and taken back to trial in England. They came face to face once more with the captain they thought dead. Three were hanged and the rest were imprisoned.

Bligh was not blamed. In 1794, he was given the Society of Arts Medal for his excellent forty-two day voyage in the longboat and in 1801 was made a Fellow of the Royal Society for his services to navigation and botany. He fought in several sea battles and after the Battle of Copenhagen was personally thanked by Nelson for his bravery.

In 1805, he was made Governor of the new colony of New South Wales in Australia and immediately ran into trouble with some of the settlers who did not like the rules and taxes ordered by the Government in faraway England. Many other settlers supported the new Governor. In 1808, there was a small revolt by the first group and Bligh was deposed and imprisoned for two years, until soldiers arrived from England and restored the King's rule.

Once again, he was not blamed but was promoted to Admiral and continued in naval service until his retirement. He is buried in London, in Lambeth.

At a time when life in the Navy was very harsh, William Bligh was known to be a strict but fair commander. He was no worse than most and better than many in his treatment of sailors. He was especially careful to see that living conditions were as good as possible, that food was edible and that men were well-treated. There is no evidence at all that he was cruel or a tyrant.

It is interesting that in those early days of Pacific exploration two Cornishmen played such an important part. Wallis paved the way for Cook's voyage by bringing back important information. Bligh sailed with Cook and improved on the knowledge of the vast Pacific Ocean. It was Wallis who discovered Tahiti, the island which played such an important part in the *Bounty* mutiny.

General Sir Walter Raleigh Gilbert

When a traveller to Bodmin is still some distance from the town, he sees a tall, slim, granite obelisk towering over it. It is called the Beacon locally but its real name is the Gilbert Monument.

Sir Walter Gilbert was born in Bodmin in 1785, a descendant of the Elizabethan seaman Sir Humphrey Gilbert and his forenames show his family ties with that other great Tudor explorer and sailor, Sir Walter Raleigh. Although he had such strong links with the sea, he became a soldier in India and at fifteen was a cadet in the Bengal Infantry. Britain fought many small wars in India during the early years of occupation and in the 1850s there were several campaigns against the Sikhs. Gilbert was then a Major-General and through his conquests in Northern India became a national hero. To mark the success of his army, the Government issued a medal bearing his picture and he has the distinction of being the only General except the Duke of Wellington to have his face on a military medal.

In Victorian times, statues or memorials to famous people were popular. At Wellington, Somerset, there is an obleisk to the famous Duke. In Bodmin, it was decided to have one on the hill overlooking the town to commemorate their local hero.

The monument is one hundred and forty-four feet high and the story of his Sikh and Afghan wars is written on the four sides of the base. Some of the lettering is now very worn. In 1854, he was an important hero but these days, perhaps the old campaigns in distant India do not seem very important any more.

The Beacon, Bodmin. A memorial to Lt. General Sir Walter Raleigh Gilbert.

John Pollard

Born in 1787 at Kingsand on the Cornish side of the Tamar, he had an undistinguished career in the Royal Navy except for one famous incident. He was the author of the most famous signal in our history. As the ships of Nelson's fleet sailed towards the enemy at the start of the Battle of Trafalgar in 1805, he was the midshipman in charge of the flag signals in the *Victory*. Nelson asked him to make the signal 'England confides that this day every man will do his duty'.

Pollard said that as 'confides' was not in the code book it would have to be spelled out, thus using a larger number of flags. He suggested that it be changed to 'expects', which was in the book. Nelson agreed, so the signal became, 'England expects that this day every man will do his duty'.

This signal has been flown many times since that famous day and is flown on Trafalgar Day each year from HMS *Victory*, now preserved as a memorial in Portsmouth. It is a proud thought that the wording was due to a Cornishman.

John Pollard rose to the rank of Commander and died in 1865.

John Carter

Not every famous Cornish sailor was in the navy, or even respectable. John Carter, known as 'The King of Prussia', was a curious mixture of honest merchant, hardworking fisherman and clever rogue. He was born in 1770, at Breage near Helston, in an area notorious for its lawless gangs of smugglers and wreckers.

Few people in the eighteenth century thought smuggling was a crime. They objected to paying money to the king when they bought such things as wine, spirits, tobacco and lace imported from abroad. They were glad to buy them more cheaply from daring smugglers who brought them in at night to lonely coves and beaches. The smugglers knew the risks of being shot or captured by the king's revenue officers but every successful cargo brought them a large profit.

Carter carried on his fishing and smuggling from Bessie's Cove, a small rocky inlet in the cliffs near Perranuthnoe in Mount's Bay. He and his brother Henry were well-known in the ports along the French coast and even during wars between England and France, they carried on a trade, although they were arrested and imprisoned for a year in St Malo on one occasion.

John became so daring and so confident as a smuggler that he even mounted guns on the cliffs above Bessie's Cove and once fired them at revenue boats which came too close. On another occasion, he raided the Customs House at Penzance and carried off some wine barrels which had been seized from his boat. As he saw himself as an honest man, he took only his own from the large number there.

In 1807, he disappeared from the area and his 'fort' was destroyed. Nothing more is known of him. He left a journal in which he related his life and adventures.

His nickname, 'The King of Prussia', was given to him because his boyhood hero was Frederick the Great, King of Prussia, a great soldier. The cove, which consists of Bessie's Cove and another next to it, is now known as Prussia Cove.

The Voyage of the *Mystery*

In 1854, the people of Cornwall were poor and distressed. There was little work and money was scarce. Thousands of men went abroad, to work in the mines of America, South Africa and Australia. Gold had been discovered in great quantities in Australia in 1851, leading to the Australian Gold Rush. Between 1852 and 1857, tens of thousands of men flocked there to find a fortune. Few did, but they all went with great hopes and were willing to travel in terrible conditions aboard ships of all kinds.

Seven Newlyn fishermen, Richard Nicholls, Job Kelynack, William and Richard Badcock, Charles Boase, P. C. Matthews and Lewis Lewis, decided to sail there in their own boat, a thirty-six foot fishing lugger called the *Mystery*. She had two masts, each carrying a lugsail and when used for fishing she had neither deck nor cabin. Like all the Mount's Bay luggers, she was very seaworthy and fast but was never intended for ocean travel.

For this voyage she was fitted with decking and a small cabin. All the fishing gear was left behind so that she could carry plenty of food and water.

One day in November, 1854, when the weather was cold and raw and the sky full of scudding dark clouds, all the people of the village assembled on the tiny horseshoe-shaped pier to watch them leave. Many, of course, thought them quite mad to go in such a cockleshell but they were all experienced fishermen and the skipper, Richard Nicholls had made many deepwater voyages. After the singing of a hymn and prayers for their safety, they left Newlyn, their brown sails disappearing from sight over the horizon.

In eight days they reached Madeira and after thirty-five days they had crossed the Atlantic to Trinidad. Here, they turned south-east and headed for Capetown, taking full advantage of the winds which blew steadily at that time of the year.

On 17 January 1855, they reached Capetown, where they were greeted with amazement. They stayed a week, taking on fresh supplies and making ready for the most dangerous part of the voyage across the southern Indian Ocean. They kept to the latitude of forty degrees south, where they were assured of strong westerly winds, although they knew they could expect storms. Once or twice, the weather was so bad that they had to ride out the gales, using a sea-anchor, or a raft of planks and barrels tied together, to keep them heading into the waves.

On a fine day in March they arrived in Melbourne after one hundred and fifteen days at sea, to be greeted as heroes. They sold the boat and divided the money and parted company to find work and fortune. It would be pleasant to record that they became millionaires but it was not to be and five of them eventually returned to

A plaque commemorating the voyage of the Mystery

Cornwall as passengers in a much larger ship. Boase died in 1874, at the early age of forty, but William Badcock survived to the age of eighty-five, dying in Newlyn in 1906. Sadly the skipper, Richard Nicholls, was killed in an accident with a horse and cart in London.

On the wall of the Fisherman's Mission building in Newlyn there is a slate plaque commemorating this epic voyage, at the time the longest voyage known to have been made in so small a boat. At the top of the plaque is a carving of the Mystery.

In the County Museum there are some models of Cornish fishing luggers which give a good idea of what the *Mystery* was like. The success of the trip was due to the sturdiness of the boat, built to withstand the storms of the Cornish coast, the skill in navigation of the skipper, and the seamanship and determination of all the crew.

1700 miles in Open Boats

In 1923, the cargo ship *Trevessa*, owned by the Hain Steamship Comapny of St Ives, was crossing the Indian Ocean on the way from Australia to Britain. The weather was bad and Captain Foster found that the ship was becoming difficult to steer. She was not lifting easily to the waves and great seas were crashing on to the foredeck. When the amount of water in the bottom compartments was measured, it was found that the foremost hold was seriously flooded and that water was pouring in through a leak.

The pumps could not cope with the inflow and *Trevessa* settled lower and lower in the water. An S.O.S. signal was sent but there were no ships near enough to help and the crew abandoned ship in two lifeboats. Captain Foster took charge of one, with twenty men, his charts, navigation books and sextant. Chief Officer Smith took the other, with twenty-four men. When the *Trevessa* sank, they were alone in the great sea, sixteen hundred

miles from Fremantle, Australia and seventeen-hundred miles from the island of Mauritius.

It was decided to make for Mauritius. Although farther away, the winds were likely to be more favourable and there was a better chance of having rain for drinking-water. They sailed together for six days but it was difficult for two very small boats to keep together, especially during darkness. After a conference, they separated and were soon sailing and rowing alone. Food and water grew short and the already small rations had to be cut again and again. Two men died in the captain's boat and nine in the chief officer's and the others must have thought that their chances of survival were slim.

Once again, however, skill, determination and seamanship won and after twenty-two days nineteen hours, the captain's boat reached Mauritius, where friendly hands helped them to safety and recovery. There was great disappointment when they found that there was no news of the other boat and it was assumed that it had been lost.

Great was their joy when, two days later, came the news that Smith's boat had arrived at the island of Rodriguez with fifteen survivors. The captain's boat had sailed over fifteen hundred miles and the chief officer's over seventeen hundred.

It was not such a long open-boat voyage as Bligh's but a great feat of endurance just the same.

The Hain Steamship Company began as a small fleet of sailing ships in the early nineteenth century, owned by a St Ives captain called Edward Hain. The company grew and prospered and became one of the country's foremost cargo-ship companies. For many years it was managed from St Ives but when it grew too large for the little Cornish port, it moved to London. All the company's ships carried Cornish names beginning with 'Tre...'. In 1917, the shares were bought by the P & O company but Hain's continued to operate under the original colours and names.

There are several reminders of the Hain Line in St Ives, particularly the Sir Edward Hain Memorial Hospital.

John Arnold

When Samuel Wallis and William Bligh navigated through the uncharted Pacific seas, they were able to fix their positions fairly accurately because they had reliable and accurate chronometers. Earlier seamen knew how to use the movements of the sun and stars to find out where they were but because they could not be exact about the times of their observations their calculations could only be approximate.

We are used to clocks and watches which keep precise time for months or even years but in those days mechanisms were crude and were often seriously affected by temperature and the movements of the ships.

It was a Bodmin man, John Arnold, who perfected the ship's chronometer and revolutionized the science of navigation in the eighteenth century. His father was a watchmaker in the town and when he was old enough he became his apprentice. They lived and worked in a narrow passage off Fore Street and watch repairing is still carried on near the spot to this day.

John became a highly skilled craftsman and went to London, where he was able to work with the best in the land and have access to the finest tools and workshops. He made a watch for King George III which was an object of marvel among the King's friends and watchmakers. At the time it was the smallest repeating watch ever made, small enough to fit into a ring for the King's finger.

He is remembered in Bodmin by a plaque over the entrance to the narrow passage where he once lived, and the name on the wall, Arnold's Passage.

Sir Humphry Davy

When we see the ruins of our old mines, we think chiefly about the miners who worked far underground and those who laboured on the surface to bring the crude ore into workable metal. There were, of course, many others who worked with neither pick nor shovel but with their brains, to improve machinery, safety and efficiency.

The talents of many Cornishmen were brought to light by the new industrial age in the eighteenth and nineteenth centuries and Davy was the leading scientist of his time. He was born on 17, December 1778, and his father was a woodcarver in Penzance. From an early age he was interested in things scientific and was fortunate in knowing Robert Duncan, a Penzance saddler who made electrical and mechanical models. The young Davy spent many absorbing hours with him. He showed talent too with words and was well-known for the writing of verse and scripts for pantomimes.

He went to school in the town and quickly showed his teachers that he had a great ability, not only with his lessons but in making mischief. No doubt they were glad when he went on to Truro Grammar School at the age of fifteen. Strangely, his headmaster there, Dr Cardew, did not see that his pupil was unusually gifted and the school did nothing to encourage his scientific knowledge. In later years, when Davy was famous, Dr Cardew said how surprised he was by it all as there had been no sign of genius when he had him as a pupil.

At sixteen, Davy became an apprentice to Dr John Borlase, a Penzance surgeon. One of his tasks was to prepare medicines and he began to use the laboratory for his own private experiments as well, learning much but putting himself and those around him in some danger as he mixed the contents of the bottles and boxes, and stirred and boiled them to see what would happen. On one occasion, in a small attic in a relative's house, he caused an explosion, causing his grandfather to say: 'This boy Humphry is incorrigible. He will surely blow us all up in the air, some day.'

Had it not been for a chance meeting with a Bristol scientist, Dr Beddoes, who came to

A statue of Sir Humphry Davy in Penzance

Cornwall with a party of scientific men, to look at the geology of the Land's End district, it is probable that the young Davy would have stayed for ever in Penzance and been unknown outside the town.

Dr Beddoes, however, was very impressed and offered him a job as assistant in his newly-opened Pneumatic Institution in Bristol. Within four years his brilliant career was established, although his experiments with gases almost cost him his life before he started. In order to test their effects on the human body, he daringly sniffed newly-discovered ones and poisoned himself so badly that he had to return to Penzance to get well.

Many honours came to him. He wrote scientific books, gave lectures, was Secretary of the Royal Society, and its President for seven years. He was knighted in 1812.

In that year came the event which was to make him known to ordinary people. An explosion at Feeling Colliery near Sunderland killed eighty-nine miners. Coal-mines were dangerous places because gas from the coal built up in the confined spaces underground and was easily ignited by a spark or by the candles used by the miners. A Society for the Prevention of Accidents in Coal Mines was formed and Davy was asked to devise some kind of safety lamp.

The result was both simple and practical. The flame of an oil lamp was enclosed in a casing of wire gauze. The air passed through the holes to feed the flame but the dangerous explosive gases were held back. Had he patented his invention he could have made a fortune but he did not do so, choosing to leave the way open for anybody to use his idea and improve on it if they could.

Davy had many other interests besides science.

He continued his youthful interest in poetry and the poet Coleridge said that had he chosen to be a poet instead of a scientist, he could have become equally famous. Fishing was another hobby from boyhood and he wrote a number of books on the subject. Few people, probably, know that it was Davy who started the Zoological Society, best known to millions for the zoo in Regent's Park, London.

He died in Switzerland in May, 1829, at the early age of fifty-one, a great loss to science. His statue stands in Market Jew Street, Penzance, near the house in which he lived, and shows him holding his Davy lamp.

William Bickford

Cornish mines had no problem with explosive gases but our miners were often killed or maimed by the misuse or faulty operation of gunpowder.

Early fuses were made from tubes of reeds or goose feathers filled with powder and were so unreliable that men were sometimes unable to get away fast enough after the fuse had been lit. At other times the fuses burned so slowly and unevenly that miners were killed by explosions when they returned to investigate a delay. Blind and badly crippled miners who had been injured by misfires were once a common sight in mining villages.

A leather merchant in Illogan, William Bickford, was watching a rope-maker spinning his threads when it occurred to him that if a strand of yarn impregnated with gunpowder were included in the rope, it might make a reliable fuse. After experiments, he produced one which worked with a flame burning at a controlled rate. He called his fuses 'Safety Rods' and in 1831 took out a patent for them and opened a factory in Tuckingmill, Camborne.

Making them was one thing; getting miners to use them was another. Many men preferred to take chances with the older and cheaper ones. Common sense won in the end and within a few years, there were other factories making the Bickford fuses.

Sir Goldsworthy Gurney

When he died in 1875, he had no money and was laid to rest in a simple grave just by the door of Launcells Church, near Bude. A sad reward for so brilliant a man.

He was born at Treator, by Padstow, in 1793, and became a surgeon in Wadebridge. His real interest lay with things mechanical and in 1823 he gave up medicine to carry out experiments with steam-engines and locomotives. He made a steam-driven boat and tried his ideas on steam-driven coaches. In 1829, one of them travelled from London to Bath and back at fifteen miles an hour, and two years later, another ran between Gloucester and Cheltenham five times daily for four months, carrying three thousand passengers for four thousand miles without serious trouble or accident.

No doubt he thought his idea would revolutionize road transport. Powerful forces fought against him, however. The sellers of coach-horses and those who provided harness and stables did not want his ideas. The owners of the many toll roads did not want steam carriages either. By raising the charges for them, they forced them off the road and Gurney was almost ruined.

He carried on with his experiments and developed one idea which was later used by George Stephenson in his locomotive *Rocket*. One of the problems with the early locomotives was that the movement forward tended to cut off the air flow to the firebox, with the result that either the fire went out or refused to burn properly. Gurney channelled air through the funnel and solved the difficulty.

Gurney invented a better form of lighting for lighthouses. He proposed a system of flashing lights for them so that sailors could identify them. Between 1854 and 1863, he was in charge of the heating, lighting and ventilating of the House of Commons, for which he was knighted in 1863. He built Bude Castle, to prove that a house could be built successfully on sand by using a concrete raft to support it.

He was a genius but his real worth was not recognized until after his death and Cornwall has no fitting memorial to him.

Richard Trevithick

Most history books tell us that George Stephenson was the father of the railways and give the impression that he invented the very first locomotive to travel on rails. This great engineer did start the railway network of passenger and freight-carrying trains which eventually covered the entire kingdom, with the opening of the railway between Stockton and Darlington in 1821 but there were engines running on the roads and on rails before that.

On Christmas Eve, 1801, a large and somewhat frightened crowd stood on the slopes of Camborne Hill as an iron-wheeled monster belching smoke and sparks from its tall chimney clanked and groaned its slow way up the steep hill. Although they were used to seeing stationary steam-engines at work in the mine engine-houses, it was new to see one moving itself by its own power.

Camborne Hill was the steepest in the district and horses had difficulty in pulling loaded wagons up it. This is remembered in the famous Cornish folk song:

> Goin' up Camborne Hill, comin' down,
> Goin' up Camborne Hill, comin' down,
> The 'osses stood still,
> The wheels went around,
> Goin' up Camborne Hill, comin' down,

Amid cheers, the engine reached the top and the engineers wiped the sweat from their blackened faces. They had proved that a steam engine could do it. It was another triumph for its inventor, Richard Trevithick, or Cap'n Dick as he was generally known. In the weeks that followed, the engine roamed the usually quiet lanes around Camborne and Redruth, scaring the wits out of many country-folk and grazing animals. Sadly, the machine came to an unfortunate end when the boiler-water boiled away while the drivers were at an inn. The engine was damaged beyond repair.

Trevithick was born in 1771 in the hamlet of Tregajorran between Camborne and Redruth. His father was Manager at Dolcoath Mine and it was natural that the boy should show interest in mechanical things. As an appentice, he had a natural genius for machines and pumps and became well-known in all the mining district of Cornwall. As an adult engineer, he knew all the engineering giants of the day and worked with many of them to improve machinery, but his passion was for locomotion, the use of steam-power for propulsion.

Three years after his Camborne Hill experiment, he built and successfully tested another engine which ran on rails at Merthyr Tydfil in Wales, pulling loaded trucks and seventy men for ten miles.

Richard Trevithick's statue in Camborne

In London, where Euston Station now stands, he had an engine and coaches running around a circular track inside a high fence, charging a fee for the privilege of travelling by 'mechanical horse', behind his engine called *Catch-Me-Who-Can*.

He was a man whose ideas followed one another with great speed and no sooner had he invented one thing than he turned his attention to another. He invented a steam threshing-machine, built a tunnel under the Thames and developed a screw propeller for driving ships. In 1816, he went to Peru to inspect and overhaul pumping engines in the mines. He stayed for eleven years, having many adventures. When he decided to come home, he had no money for the fare and it was another engineer, Robert Stephenson, who lent him the money.

Trevithick returned penniless and in poor health. He was forced to work as an ordinary engineer in London and, when he died in 1833, his friends had to collect money to save him from a pauper's grave.

He has been called the 'Cornish Giant', not only because of his gigantic talent but because he was a very tall and powerful man. There are tales of how he once hurled a heavy sledge-hammer right over an engine-house and picked up a burly miner, turned him upside-down and planted the imprints of the soles of his boots on the ceiling of a mine count-house.

There is a statue to him in Camborne, outside the public library. He is looking up Beacon Hill and holding a model of his locomotive. In Westminster Abbey there is a memorial window to this great Cornish engineer.

Richard and John Lander

At the top of Lemon Street, Truro, is a tall column on which stands the figure of Richard Lander, explorer of the River Niger.

He and his brother were born at the Fighting Cocks Inn, Truro, in 1804 and 1807, respectively. When a young man, John sailed to most countries in the world. After one voyage of discovery to West Africa in 1825 he wrote an account of it and this, together with his great experience of world travel, brought him to the notice of the government as a possible leader of expeditions.

In 1830, the Lander brothers were sent to Africa to explore the lower reaches of the great River Niger which flows hundreds of miles from the interior of what was then a mysterious and unknown continent, to the Atlantic Ocean. They charted the many separate mouths of the river and published their findings in *Journal of an Expedition to Explore the Course and Termination of the Niger.*

They made two more successful and useful expeditions but, on a third, John Lander was killed in a fight with natives. Cornwall was remembered by the brothers in naming some of the landmarks along the Niger. They called one island Truro Island and a hill, Cornwall Mountain.

A memorial at Truro to the Lander brothers

John Couch Adams

In the tiny and isolated church of Laneast in the heart of Bodmin Moor between Altarnun and Davidstow is a small memorial tablet to the memory of this great scientist who was born in the parish in 1819. He tended his father's sheep and went to the small village school, where he showed such skill in mathematics that his teacher said that he could teach him no more. His special interest was astronomy and he spent many of the night hours watching the stars and planets.

His father saw that the boy had great ability and sent him to a school at Saltash. From there he went to Cambridge and had great academic success. By the use of mathematics only, he worked out that there had to be an unknown planet out in space. A French astronomer, working separately with the same figures and facts, came to the same result. They published their discovery at the same time. The planet was called Neptune.

He became Professor of Astronomy at Cambridge in 1858 and was also Director of the University Observatory. For some reason, he refused a knighthood and also the post of Astronomer Royal, the highest honour in the land. He died in 1892.

Henry Trengrouse

When the frigate *Anson* was driven ashore on the Loe Bar, near Porthleven, on 19 December, 1807, nearly one hundred men were drowned because they were unable to cross the short distance between the wreck and the shore. It was so rough that swimming was impossible and no boats could have lived in the boiling surf. Although the beach was crowded with willing helpers, there was nothing that could be done.

Among the watchers was a Helston cabinet maker called Henry Trengrouse. He was so affected by what he had seen that he spent the rest of his life and most of his money trying to invent an apparatus which would save ship-wrecked sailors in such a situation. It is said that he was watching a fireworks display when he had the idea that if a rocket could carry a light line between shore and wreck, the sailors could use that line to pull heavier ropes aboard. They could then use the heavy rope to carry themselves through the sea to safety.

He had to work for several years before he had an apparatus which really worked. It was portable and could be carried aboard ships as well as used from the land. He offered it to the Admiralty and to Trinity House, the organization which looks after the lighthouses and buoys around the coast. At first, they were politely interested but would not give him money to develop it further. It took him ten years before the government agreed that it was a splendid idea and paid him a mere £20 for it. He probably made no more than £50 from it altogether, having spent much more than that on it himself.

Today, all ships carry a rocket life-saving apparatus and coastguards all over the world have them ready for instant use.

Trengrouse also invented a new type of life-jacket for sailors and fishermen, and built a model of an unsinkable lifeboat. Like so many bene-factors and inventors, he used his money and his health in trying to protect others and, when he died in 1854, he was penniless.

John Opie, The Cornish Wonder

Born about 1770, the son of the village carpenter in the village of Mithian near St Agnes, John Opie was very popular with his friends and the adults of the village. He could draw the most marvellous portraits of them and his skill was known for miles around.

The ability to draw did not earn a living for any poor person in those days and when he was about twelve he became his father's apprentice, mending gates and doors, making tables and cupboards and learning how to use the carpenter's tools.

One day, while working with his father in the house of a wealthy man, he was found copying one of the portraits hanging on the walls. The owner was amazed by the boy's skill, especially when he learned that he had never had a single lesson and had seen very few pictures of any kind. He therefore encouraged him and gave him paper and pencils and allowed him to use the family portraits as models. His parents were far from pleased. They thought he should not waste time on such useless rubbish as drawing pictures.

He was sawing logs in his father's yard when he was visited by Dr Wolcot from Truro, a man who befriended and encouraged many young people with talent, and who had many friends in London's artistic circle. He offered to take John into his own house and give him an education.

The Opies reluctantly agreed and the boy was taken into a new world of studying, reading, writing, mathematics and science. He was also learning the techniques of drawing and painting. Many rich people in Truro were pleased to have their portraits painted by him.

When Opie was about twenty, Dr Wolcot took him to London and introduced him to the famous painter Sir Joshua Reynolds, President of the Royal Academy. 'Here is my Cornish Wonder,' he said.

In 1782 his work was shown at the Royal Academy, a great honour for any artist, but especially so for the son of a poor Cornish carpenter. For about twenty years he was the most fashionable portrait painter in London, completing more than seven hundred pictures. He also gave lectures and wrote several books. It seemed that he was destined to become one of the greatest men in the country but unfortunately he died in 1807, after a short illness. He had the honour of being buried in St Paul's Cathedral.

Henry Bone

A painter of a different kind, he was born in Truro in 1755. In 1771 he was apprenticed to William Cookworthy, the owner and founder of the Plymouth China Works, where porcelain was made following Cookworthy's discovery of the huge china-clay deposits around St Austell.

When Cookworthy opened his Bristol Porcelain Works, he employed Bone in painting designs and pictures on very small porcelain buttons and brooches. In 1778, Bone went to London and used his great skill in painting in watercolours on ivory and enamel. So great was his ability that he became the official enamel painter to the Prince of Wales in 1800, and from 1801 to his death in 1854, enamellist to the King. His eldest son, Henry Pierce Bone, inherited his skill and interest and was enamellist to Queen Adelaide and to Queen Victoria.

Neville Northey Burnard

Another genius from the Cornish countryside, he was born in 1818 at Altarnun, where his father was a stonemason. Slate was the common material for tombstones and he showed great skill in carving. When he was very young he won a silver medal at the Royal Cornwall Polytechnic Exhibition in 1834. Sir Charles Lemon, one of the leading citizens in Truro, took an interest in him and sent him to London where he met the leading sculptors of the time and became an able sculptor himself.

His works in Cornwall range from a tombstone just inside the door of St Petroc's Church in Bodmin, to a bust of John Wesley at Altarnun and the noble statue of John Lander at Truro.

His great weakness was his over-fondness for alcohol and his work declined in quality and quantity. He became destitute and when he returned to Cornwall, heartbroken after the death of his daughter in 1875, he soon fell into debt and ruin. He ended his days as a pauper in Redruth workhouse in 1878, having wasted his genius.

**Newlyn Art Gallery.
The round plaques above the name
are of beaten copper.**

The 'Newlyn School' of Artists

In the late years of the nineteenth century, a number of artists settled in Newlyn and founded a group dedicated to the painting of realistic pictures from the scenes they saw around them. This was something of a new idea in this country, the artists having being inspired by new thinking abroad, particularly in France.

They came to Newlyn because the fishing boats and the local people made such good subjects and because the light was so good and the climate favourable to painting out-of-doors. They rejected the painting of imaginary scenes in the comfort of a warm studio and set up their easels in the streets and on the pier. One said jokingly: 'Your work cannot be really good unless you have caught a cold doing it.'

At first, they were regarded with amusement or hostility. Many Newlyn people thought they were quite mad. Others thought their work sinful and their way of life even more so. However, they paid their models and in such a poor community even a few coppers were welcome. Their finished paintings showed the boats, the harbour, the cottages and local people going about their work. Before long they had become accepted as part of Newlyn life. Between 1880 and 1900 the 'Newlyn School' was regarded as the freshest approach to painting in the whole country.

No fashion lasts for ever and, after about 1900, the colony got smaller. The 1914-1918 war made further changes inevitable but for many years Newlyn was known as The Artists' Town, and art is still very much a part of its life.

Paintings by the original artists are now highly priced and it is not too much to say that in time, they will become as sought-after and valuable as Rembrandt and Vermeer. The name most associated with The Newlyn School is that of A. Stanhope Forbes. Although not one of the original members, he was one of the leading painters and stayed in the village until his death in 1947 at the age of ninety, having first arrived in 1884. His wife Elizabeth was a leading water-colour artist and together, in 1899, they started a teaching school for would-be painters. Forbes was a well-liked and respected figure in Newlyn and was a familiar sight, with his easel strapped to the frame of his bicycle. Many a Newlyn boy, proudly showing his mother a picture he had drawn, was patted on the head and called 'Stanhope Forbes'.

Although none of these artists was Cornish, they became Cornish by adoption and their work should be included in any history of Cornwall.

'Q' and Other Cornish Writers

A strange name, 'Q'. An abbreviation for Sir Arthur Quiller-Couch, one of Cornwall's greatest writers and scholars. Born in Bodmin in 1863, he went to Oxford and wrote many novels, short stories and articles. He made his home in Fowey, at a house called 'The Haven', and many of his stories are set in and around the harbour. He was passionately proud of Cornwall and became a leading figure in Cornish politics and Cornish organizations. He was knighted in 1910 and was Professor of English Literature at Cambridge for thirty-two years. 'Q' *was* Cornwall and to read his Cornish stories on a cold, dark and wet winter's day brings back memories of all that is best in a Cornish summer, its sights and smells, its colours and sounds, and its charms before the growth of the tourist trade.

Many excellent Cornish writers are still alive and not only producing books but broadcasting on radio and television. Charles Causley, a teacher at Launceston for many years, is well-known for his poetry and his work in broadcasting in the south-west. Jack Clemo, poet and story-teller, is all the more remarkable because he is both blind and deaf. He suffered his first attack of blindness at the age of five and became permanently blind in 1953 when he was thirty-seven. At eighteen, he became deaf but his brave response to the challenge of his handicaps and his memories of the clay area around St Austell have produced much fine literary work. He lives near St Austell, where he was born.

Undoubtedly, the greatest living Cornish scholar and writer is Alfred Leslie Rowse. He has achieved the highest academic honours at Oxford and Cambridge Universities and is the leading historian of the Elizabethan age. His writings range from the most learned biographies and histories to stories and poetry.

Born into a family of clay-workers and shop-keepers at St Austell in 1903 he won what was then a most remarkable success for a child from a working-class family–graduation from the village school and local secondary school to a place at Christ Church College, Oxford. Those who have been brought up in the present days of many universities and colleges, with grants of money by the government to students, can have little idea of the difficulties he faced in his early years. Then, university education was for the rich and privileged sons of upper-class families. It was almost unheard for anybody else. Only outstanding ability and a dogged perseverance enabled him to win success. Happily, he remains a true Cornishman and although his work keeps him out of Cornwall a great deal, his real home is still near St Austell.

Jonathan Trelawny

Kept till last is the story of Jonathan Trelawny, the hero of the rousing song *Trelawny,* or *The Song of the Western Men,* long regarded as Cornwall's national anthem and sung with spirit on important Cornish occasions.

He and his family came from Pelynt and we have read the epitaph to one of his lawyer relatives. When the Duke of Monmouth landed in Dorset in 1685 to lead a rebellion against King James II, he organized loyal support for the king in the west. In 1688 he was one of seven bishops who were imprisoned in the Tower of London and tried for their lives for refusing to sign a paper which would have brought back Roman

Catholicism as the official religion of the country. They said that they were loyal to the King but their consciences would not allow them to sign such a document. James said that 'My Lord of Bristol was the sauciest of the seven'.

To the King's annoyance the seven men were acquitted and freed. A few weeks later he was sent into exile and William of Orange became King William III. In these last weeks of his reign, James tried to regain Trelawny's support by offering him the Bishopric of Exeter but the bishop supported William. Who can blame him?

He did become Bishop of Exeter in the following year and died in 1721 as Bishop of Winchester. More than a hundred years later, Richard Stephen Hawker, the Vicar of Morwenstow, adapted an old song to record Trelawny's stand against King James and many people believe that it was actually sung at the time. It begins:

> A good sword and a trusty hand
> A merry heart and true,
> King James's men shall understand
> What Cornish lads can do.
>
> And have they fixed the where and when?
> And shall Trelawny die?
> Here's twenty thousand Cornishmen
> Will know the reason why.

In Pelynt church we can see his chair and his bishop's crook.

No man decides for himself that he will become famous. He can choose to be a tinker, a tailor or a candlestick-maker but only his fellow men will give him fame and often this award comes long after his death.

Some of those mentioned here died without knowing that future generations would build statues or erect plaques to their memory. Some even died in poverty, having received no material reward for their efforts. A few won a place in society during their lifetime. Only the future will show which of our present generation will be considered as famous Cornishmen.

Some Things To Do

1 Visit the birthplaces of the famous people described here and see if you can find out more about them.

2 Those famous people mentioned are only a few. Can you discover more?

3 Read more about the times these famous people lived in. It will help you to see them more clearly.

Bishop Trelawny's chair in Pelynt church

Chapter 9

SOME CORNISH CUSTOMS AND TRADITIONS

Before the car and aeroplane enabled people to travel far from their homes for excursions and holidays, and before radio and television kept them indoors during the winter, they made their own amusements. Besides the usual calendar of months and days, there was the local calendar of events, known to all and eagerly awaited and prepared for. Every village and town celebrated ancient customs and traditions, many of them so old that nobody knew their true origin. They had been handed down from generation to generation and it is certain that many were relics of pagan Celtic days. Whatever their origin, they gave everybody a chance to take part in social life and something to talk about during the dark days of winter when the family gathered around the fire.

Some of the customs are still kept but most have disappeared from ordinary life. Once a tradition is dropped, it rarely is revived and, apart from the changes in people's lifestyles, two great wars this century caused the abandonment of much that was traditional.

In Cornwall, the local feast day used to be a great occasion. This was an annual holiday to celebrate the life of the parish saint. It was one of the few days in the year when nobody did any work. Scores, if not hundreds, of men, women and children flocked to the village from the surrounding countryside, to take part in games and races, to see the sideshows and to buy from the stalls set up in the square. The hounds met in the morning, dogs, riders and spectators all packing the street by the village inn; the games took part in the afternoon and there was drinking and dancing in the evening. Even young children were allowed to stay up late on feast day. Luxuries were to be had in plenty on that day, sweet buns known as 'fancies', toffee-apples, nuts, raisins, sweets and sugared almonds; to say nothing of mountains of ordinary fare, pasties, saffron cake and buns, all washed down by gallons of hot tea by the more respectable people, and gallons of ale by those considered to be 'sinners'.

For many, feast days were the only chance to spend a few hard-earned coppers on luxuries or to enjoy a whole day's entertainment for very little cost. In West Cornwall, at least, Madron Feast, St Just Feast and Paul Feast are still celebrated although they are all shadows of what they used to be like.

Sunday school galas, or outings, were also popular and each kind of church tried to make its gala the best. Only those who attended regularly were allowed to come so it was a good way of keeping up attendances on Sundays. Great was the boasting at school on the following day about the fun that was had and the food that was consumed, and great was the envy of those who had not been there.

Before the days of motor transport it was the custom for all the children and parents to assemble at the church or chapel early in the morning, dressed in their best clothes, and to walk a mile or two to the estate of the local landowner. After a speech of welcome, there were three cheers for the host and the serious business of the day began-the games and the tea. When buses became a popular means of transport, many children were taken to the seaside a few miles away, perhaps their only trip to the sea for the whole year.

'School treat buns' were eagerly looked for on these occasions. Saffron buns fully six inches across and filled with currants were given away with large mugs of tea, filling even the emptiest stomach. Sadly, they are a thing of the past but still very fondly remembered by many older people.

If the great day of the parish church was the feast day of its patron saint, the great day in the Methodist year was Anniversary Sunday, the annual remembrance of its founding. There were special services with important and fiery speakers, concerts and parades through the streets, and all the girls and ladies wore new hats and dresses.

In days when drunkedness was a great problem and many men squandered their small wages on beer, the Temperance Societies flourished and they too had their annual celebrations. There was great competition for the honour of carrying the banner or even just holding on to the long tassels which streamed from it. A number of these 'Band of Hope' banners still exist although they are no longer seen in the streets.

A love of singing has always been a Cornish characteristic and at one time there were many village bands and choirs. Every church and chapel had a large choir. Nobody stayed away from practices as there were too many others willing to take vacant places. To be in the choir was an honour not given up easily. Cornwall still has many fine choirs and bands and some have achieved national fame. To have been in a Cornish chapel on a Sunday evening and to have heard the opening hymn thundered out by a packed congregation and choir, with all the parts rendered in harmony, is an experience never to be forgotten. Such singing was all the more remarkable because few of those present had any knowledge of written music. Their ability to harmonize was a natural one, a Celtic trait, still seen and heard to the full in Wales and Cornwall.

A custom which dates back to pre-Christian times is Padstow's 'Obby 'Oss celebration on 1 May each year. It still attracts thousands of spectators. Early in the morning, the 'Obby 'Oss, a fearsome creature with a tall pointed hat, a ferocious face mask and a black tarpaulin body appears in the narrow streets. To the music of the traditional song, which everybody recognizes but which few can hum afterwards, it dances through the town after the 'Teaser', who entices it with his staff. We should say, 'her' staff because the figure is that of a woman, although the part has traditionally been taken by a man. During the rest of the year, the 'Obby 'Oss lives in a public house by the harbour and a message in Cornish over the front door proclaims the fact. This ceremony has often been accompanied by a good deal of unruly behaviour and this, as well as its undoubted pagan origins, has caused some well-meaning people to try to have it banned. However, it seems to be as firmly fixed as ever and is one tradition which is likely to go on for a long time yet.

The celebration of May Day, marking the change of the season from dark winter to joyous summer, was celebrated by other cermonies, too. Children used to rise early in the day and take to the streets blowing whistles and trumpets, carrying branches of sycamore and greenery.

Helston Furry Day, on 8 May, is another traditional ceremony still celebrated. It is often called, quite wrongly, Helston Flora Day. "Furry" comes from a Latin word 'feriae', meaning a festival day. This particular day is a Feast Day of St Michael, the patron saint of Cornwall and also the patron saint of Helston. The day used to begin with the May Day ceremony of the Hal-an-Tow, when branches of greenery were collected and used to decorate the houses. May Day and the May Feast of St Michael are so close together that the two ceremonies have been mixed and the Hal-an-Tow part largely forgotten.

In the dancing on Furry Day, elegantly dressed couples dance through the streets, and once danced in and out of the houses as well, to celebrate the completion of the Hal-an-Tow.

Another pre-Christian festival takes place on Midsummer Eve, when large bonfires are lit in a chain from Land's End to the Tamar. The original belief was that they were in honour of the sun god on the day when the sun reaches its highest point in the sky. Preparations are made well in advance as there is considerable labour in dragging bushes, logs and burnable rubbish to the tops of the highest hills. A ceremony precedes the lighting. The words, 'We do as our fathers did before us' are spoken in Cornish and a garland of herbs and flowers is thrown into the flames when the torch is applied. It was once the custom to drive animals through the flames and for men and women to leap through them, in the belief that this had the effect of driving away evil spirits.

A good summer meant a good harvest and security for the winter. When the last handful of corn was cut it was the custom for the reaper to hold it aloft and cry out, 'We 'ave 'un'. The rest of the workers shouted, 'What 'ave 'ee?', to which the reply was, 'A neck, A neck'. This was the signal for general rejoicing and celebration of a job well done. In recent years, the ceremony of Crying the Neck has been revived on some farms, although the use of machinery now makes harvest so much quicker and easier.

Christmas was celebrated with family parties, carol-singing and the decoration of churches and houses with garlands and wreaths. The traditional Christmas tree in Cornwall is the holly, a fact remembered in the carol, *The Holly and the Ivy*. This old song was written down at the dictation of an old man in St Day village, and was given the name the St Day Carol.

Between Christmas and Twelfth Night was the season for the guise dancers, parties of young people dressed in weird costumes who roamed the streets and sometimes acted the old mummers' play of St George and the Dragon. This ancient play, which has in it such unlikely characters as Father Christmas and a comic doctor, as well as a Turkish knight, the King of Egypt's daughter and St George, was once performed all over the country. One can still hear old people refer to anybody dressed in strange costume as 'looking like guise dancers'.

Twelfth Night, the end of Christmas, was celebrated with parties and the ceremonial burning of the Christmas decorations on the fire accompanied by the singing of traditional songs. It was considered most unlucky to keep the decorations after this time.

Hurling the Silver Ball is still observed in St Ives and St Columb. In St Ives it takes place on Feast Monday. The ball is thrown to the waiting crowd by the Mayor and is tossed from hand to hand along the beach. Whoever holds it when the time limit expires is the winner of the prize. In St Columb it takes place on Shrove Tuesday and is played in the streets. These are not games for the gentle. There is much pushing and pulling and not a few bruises are collected, but all in good fun.

Wrestling was a popular sport throughout Britain and in the Celtic countries it was especially so. It is not the kind of wrestling seen on television today. Cornish wrestlers wear a short jacket and each man holds tightly to the other's jacket with one hand while attempting to get a throw. There is much use of the legs and feet to try to hook the opponent's legs to throw him off balance.

The Cornish were such noted wrestlers that many visitors to the county made a point of writing about them. Richard Carew wrote in 1602 that there was hardly a place in Cornwall where expert wrestlers could not be found among the boys and young men and it is said that at the Battle of Agincourt in 1415, the Cornishmen in the army of Henry V carried a banner showing two wrestlers in action. In times past, the best local wrestler was a hero and matches were attended by many hundreds of spectators, all eager to bet on the outcome. Wrestling in the Cornish style may still be seen at local fairs and events but is no longer as common as it was. All kinds of people took part. It was very popular among miners but one of the finest wrestlers was a parson of the seventeenth century, the Rev. Richard Stevens, Headmaster of Truro Grammar School.

All these occasions were grand excuses for much eating and drinking. Traditional Cornish dishes were simple. They had to be, as few people had more than a small amount of money. Ale was brewed at home and was once the regular drink of all. Tea was unknown until the sixteenth century and it was a long time before it became cheap enough to become available to even the poorest. Strangely, once available, it became so popular in Cornwall that nearly every house kept the teapot simmering on the hob for instant use in case of visitors. The true Cornishman does not take sugar in his tea, except when eating pasties. Perhaps this comes from the days when sugar was so expensive that in poor Cornwall it could only be afforded on special occasions.

The pasty, now seen in some awful disguises, started life as a tasty and nourishing meal which could be taken underground, into the fields or in a boat, anywhere where there were no cooking facilities. It is at least as tasty cold as when hot. The traditional filling was potatoes and turnip, with meat if available. The correct way to eat one is to hold it in the hand and work one's way from one end to the other. To ensure that nobody else ate a piece left for later consumption it was the custom to mark one end with the initial of the owner. Needless to say, the eater began at the other end.

It has been said, with some truth, that nobody can make a Cornish pasty unless they are Cornish and have been taught the art by a Cornish expert. Many non-Cornish people try, but somehow their efforts never have the right taste and appearance. The shape depends on the 'crimping' of the pastry when closing the pasty, and this is an art. Improperly done, the pasty opens up during the cooking. Cooks from 'up-the-country' often refuse to believe that raw materials, meat, potatoes and turnip, will cook at the same rate inside a pastry case and commit the awful sin of using pre-cooked minced beef. Such things may be called Cornish pasties but they certainly are nothing of the kind.

Mention of the pasty reminds us of another piece of Cornish folklore, the existence of the fear-some Bucca. He appears in various disguises and in different places–underground in the mines, and at sea. No doubt, old Cornish people thought of him as the Devil but gave him their own special name.

In the mines, there were always unexplained noises. The tapping of hammers could be heard, the wind in the tunnels made sighing sounds and the flickering of the candles made strange shadows dance on the walls. Superstitious miners believed it was the Bucca, watching them and planning some mischief. To keep him happy, it was the custom to leave the corner of a pasty for him and, since the food often disappeared before the next 'core', it was proof enough of his existence. Fishermen, too, saw the hand of the Bucca in the storms and in the lack of success they frequently had.

In Newlyn, by Penzance, there is a road known to older residents as Bucca's Pass and not far away is a large outcrop of rock called Devil's Rock. Legend says that the Bucca came from the sea and landed on the rock before being chased away over the fields by the vicar and choir of Paul church, chanting hymns and psalms. Certain marks in the rock can be identified as having been made by the Bucca's cup, spoon and net.

If the Bucca was huge, the Cornish pixie, or 'pisky', was very small. Piskies were everywhere in the country and were responsible for causing hens to stop laying, cows to cease from giving milk, milk to turn sour and any other trouble which might occur. They delighted in leading travellers into bogs and thorn brakes and could cause paths to disappear. Anybody who was muddled and lost was said to be 'pisky-laden'.

A belief in little people, dwarfs and goblins, is one of man's oldest superstitions and is to be found all over the world. It has persisted in the Celtic countries and is a feature in Celtic myths and stories.

Other Cornish superstitions centred on the robin and the wren. The former was always regarded as a very unlucky bird and if one persisted in coming indoors, it was seen as an omen of disaster for somebody in the house. An old saying ran as follows:

> Kill a robin or a wran (wren)
> and you'll never prosper boy or man.

To return to food, heavy cake, or hevva cake to give it its true name, has already been mentioned in the chapter on Fishing. Saffron cake is an item peculiar to Cornwall and nobody seems to know why. Saffron comes from the stamen of crocus flowers and is very expensive. 'As dear as saffern' was once a Cornish way of describing anything of high price. Legend says that it was brought to Cornwall by Phoenicians coming here for tin but, whoever introduced it, they certainly gave us something original and lasting. Years ago, saffron had another use. Made into saffron tea, it was given to thousands of children suffering from measles. It was said to 'bring out the spots'. So generations of children blessed the Phoenicians for giving them something tasty to eat and a cure for the measles.

A once cheap and popular dish was marinated pilchards. When these fish could be bought for as little as one penny for a hundred, they provided food which could be kept for weeks and used during the autumn and early winter months. The fish were laid head to tail in tin dishes, with spices, bay leaves and vinegar. Covered with brown paper and tied around with string, they were baked for several hours, filling the house with a spicy aroma. They were very tasty when cold and even the bones were edible. Alas, the pilchard has almost disappeared from our shores and marinated pilchards are rarely seen.

As we have already learned, in lean fishing seasons, winkles and limpets were collected from the rocks and used as food. It was known as tryg-meat, an interesting name coming from the Cornish word 'tryg' meaning low tide or the ebb tide, the time when such creatures could be gathered.

Starry-gazy pie is often mentioned in books on Cornwall as having been a traditional dish although it is almost impossible to find anyone who remembers having eaten it or even seen it. It seems to have originated in Mousehole. In the nineteenth century, after a very bad fishing season, when the inhabitants were on the verge of starvation, a fisherman named Tom Bawcock made a large and unexpected catch of assorted fish. Great was the rejoicing, and in celebration a pie was made, with the heads of the different kinds of fish poking through the pastry and looking upwards to the sky.

Tom Bawcock's Eve is kept in Mousehole to this day, just before Christmas, and a similar pie is served to the customers in the Ship Inn.

These are a few of our ancient customs, from more leisurely days when most people grew up, worked and died within a few miles of their birthplace; when everybody knew everybody else and when the annual customs meant a great deal. To learn more about them you must talk to those who have lived in Cornwall all their lives and who are now past eighty. These are the people who will remember taking part in the old ceremonies and can describe the enormous pleasure they gained from them.

Our ancestors may not have had the scientific marvels we now take for granted. They may not have travelled far and they may have been very superstitious but their lives were by no means dull. They were very self-reliant, independent and proud and there was a richness in their years that we no longer possess.

Some Things To Do

1 Go to Helston on Furry Day and Padstow on 'Obby 'Oss Day.

2 Are there any local customs where you live?

3 Ask some of the older people in your family what customs and traditions they remember.

4 Go to a midsummer bonfire when the time comes.

Chapter 10

CORNISH CASTLES AND CORNISH HOMES

The oldest castles of Cornwall are the hilltop forts of the Iron Age Celts, now discernible only by the remains of banks and ditches. There are others, more obvious to the eye, built between the eleventh and the sixteenth centuries when the country was often threatened by disorder within and enemies without. The earlier ones served as defensive homes for the local overlord and fell into decay when law and order under a strong ruler spread to the farthest corners of the kingdom, and when cannon made even the strongest walls quite useless. The later ones, built to defend the coast against a possible invader, were no longer needed when the danger passed and have been kept intact as national monuments. Only one is still a family home and that has a history which is unique.

When William the Conqueror became King of England he united what had been little more than a collection of small kingdoms into one country. His rule quickly extended to the borders of Wales and Scotland. Cornwall, which had been conquered by the Saxons, was no longer an independent Celtic land and came under the Norman sway. One of William's first acts was to reward those powerful barons who had helped him, with gifts of land. They were allowed to rule them in their own way, provided that they acknowledged him as supreme overlord and gave him taxes and military support when he needed it.

To his half-brother, Robert, Count of Mortain, he gave the whole of Cornwall and during the next few hundred years, Cornwall was ruled in his name by a succession of relatives of the Norman and Plantagenet kings. The first Duke of Cornwall, a title borne by the eldest son of the King or Queen, was Edward the Black Prince, son of Edward III who ruled between 1327 and 1377. There was a title, Earl of Cornwall, before this and the most important man to hold it was Richard, a brother of Henry III, 1216 to 1272. Richard, Earl of Cornwall, is believed to have been the first user of the badge of Cornwall, fifteen golden balls, or bezants, on a black shield. He owned all the major Cornish castles at one time and was responsible for a great deal of improvement to them, although he

visited them but rarely. He called himself King of the Romans and spent most of his adult life abroad trying to get himself accepted as head of the Holy Roman Empire, a collection of states and countries originally founded by Charlemagne.

Another important man in Cornwall, also responsible for improvements to several castles, was Reginald de Dunstanville, a son of Henry I, who reigned for thirty-five years from 1100.

When Robert of Mortain came across the Tamar to inspect his new possession, he decided to make his headquarters at Launceston. It was close to England, there was a small thriving town there already at the foot of a splendid steep hill and it was altogether an ideal place. His first task was to build a fort, to impress the inhabitants with his power and within which he could be safe from attack. It has to be remembered that he and his men were invaders and there was always the chance of rebellion by the conquered people.

His workmen made the hill even steeper, dug ditches and erected a palisade fence. Inside the space so made, the bailey as it was called, they built wooden houses to serve as living quarters, stables, barracks and workshops. On the very summit of the hill they made a timber stronghold, the keep, to be a last-ditch defence should an enemy succeed in capturing the bailey below. This construction of a keep on a mound of earth, either natural or man-made, with buildings within a defensive bailey, was the typical Norman castle of the time. Scores were built all over the country. Robert's choice of Launceston, or Dunheved as it was called then, was an important one for Cornwall. For the next nine hundred years, the town was the capital of the county, until its position at the far east of the peninsula made it unsuitable to the changing needs of government, and Bodmin was chosen as the county town instead.

When he died in 1090, the castle was still much as he built it and it was not until about 1150 that the new owner, Reginald de Dunstanville, began to replace the timber defences with stone. His work has now almost disappeared. The ruined castle we see today is the work of Richard, Earl of

Cornwall. He not only wished to make a strong and impressive fortress but a fine home for himself as well. We know that when the work was finished, he took his wife there for the honeymoon, so obviously he was very proud of it.

Passing through various hands, by the sixteenth century it was in ruins. The walls had fallen in many places, the local townspeople had taken much of the stone to build houses, walls and barns. Pigs had invaded the bailey and caused damage to the foundations by rooting at the base of the walls. Ivy covered the stonework so that it was difficult to find. Whenever there was revolt in the land, repairs were made but as soon as peace came nobody bothered to restore it.

When the Civil War came to Cornwall the castle was hastily fortified by the Cornish Royalists and it then saw its only military use. It was besieged by the army of Parliament and held out for a short time, until battered into surrender by their artillery. From then on it fell into even greater ruin and was not rescued until the reign of Queen Victoria, when the bailey was laid out as a public park and the remaining walls partly restored.

During its life it earned itself the name of Castle Terrible and a reputation of being an evil place. The gaol was an awful dungeon and many prisoners suffered and died there. The walls dripped water all the time, there was little or no light, and rats kept the prisoners company, sharing their meagre food. Even when the castle was so ruinous as to be uninhabitable, a prison remained in the Doomsdale Tower, so called because few who entered came out alive. The remains of this tower can still be seen and on the walls there are plaques to the memories of its two most famous prisoners.

Cuthbert Mayne was a Jesuit priest in the reign of Elizabeth I. In 1575 he came from France to live at the great houses of Lanherne and Golden, homes of the powerful Arundell family. In and around these two houses he preached the Catholic faith and conducted religious services for the Arundells and other Catholic families in the area. Today, there would be nothing remarkable about this but then it all had to be done in the utmost secrecy, for to be a Catholic was to be a potential traitor to the country.

In the 1570s, there was only one official Christian religion in Europe and the forms of its services and beliefs were ordered by the Pope in Rome. To offend the Pope, to attempt to alter the official doctrines in any way, was to be declared a heretic and so be liable to severe punishment, even death. In 1570, Queen Elizabeth quarrelled with the Pope and was declared by him to be a heretic. This automatically made her an enemy of all Catholics and every Catholic in Britain thus became suspect. Their religious services were forbidden and anyone found to be in possession of Catholic objects or books was arrested.

So, Cuthbert Mayne came in secret, worked in secret and lived in hiding, fearful of every knock at the door. Those who sheltered him were in equal danger. His presence in Cornwall was suspected and in the summer of 1577, Richard Grenville, then Sheriff of Cornwall, came to Golden with a party of armed men and searched the house. They found Mayne in hiding and with him a collection of forbidden objects. He was arrested and taken to the filthy prison at Launceston Castle while the owner of the house, Tregian, a member of the Arundell family by marriage, was hauled before the bishop and questioned. Released on bail of £2,000, Grenville immediately took him into custody also and conveyed him to Launceston.

The result of the investigation which followed was that a large number of people, great and small, were brought before the courts and punished. For Mayne, the penalty was extreme. On St Andrew's Day, 30 November, 1577, he was taken from the prison to the town square and executed with great brutality. Grenville was knighted for his zeal in defence of the kingdom.

The other important prisoner of Launceston was George Fox, the founder of the Quakers or, to give them their correct name, the Society of Friends. In 1656, he and two others were arrested in St Ives for distributing religious papers. They were taken to Launceston gaol and eventually brought before a court. Their offence was not a serious one but they refused to take their hats off to the judge and were therefore imprisoned until they apologised.

This they refused to do. The gaoler tried to make them pay high prices for food for themselves and their horses and since they would not do so they remained in the Doomsdale Tower for five months, in the most appalling conditions. Afterwards they were released, having proved their point with great suffering. It is said that the gaoler and his wife were themselves imprisoned in Doomsdale the following year and died there.

Tintagel Castle must be one of the most romantically sited in the country. Perched on high cliffs, with the sea on three sides, it is really two castles, one on the 'island' and the other on the mainland. There is actually no separation of the two but to go from one to the other it is necessary to descend almost to sea-level and then climb up steep stairs. We have read how it is associated with King Arthur although even the earliest parts were built long after his time. It has no exciting history and was in ruins by the sixteenth century.

Restormel Castle, at Lostwithiel, is a perfect example of a shell keep, a high circular wall enclosing a courtyard, with rooms built against the inside of the wall. The first castle there was a wooden one, built by the lord of the manor, a man with the fine-sounding name of Baldwin Fitz Turstin. Later owners replaced his timber structure with stone, building spacious rooms on the upper floor for the owner and his family. There was a great hall, a private apartment called the solar and several bedchambers. A kitchen with an enormous fireplace provided food and a well in the courtyard gave them a secure water supply. In the thirteenth century, a chapel was built on the east side and the priest lived in a wooden room fixed to the outside of the wall. Among its interesting features is a small funnel in the wall of the principal room, leading to the wall walk. It was a speaking tube, enabling messages to be passed from the battlements to the lord of the castle.

Restormel Castle

Edward the Black Prince came here several times but as far as we know its only warlike activity came during the Civil War when it was already in ruins.

Because it has a magnificent view over the surrounding country, the Parliamentary soldiers mounted artillery on top of the ruined chapel, building a strong wooden platform to take the weight of the cannon. The Royalists, under another Richard Grenville, besieged it for several days before it surrendered. A number of skeletons, some in armour, have been found here during restoration work.

The last of the Norman castles is near Saltash, at Trematon, overlooking the River Lynher. It is also a shell keep and has a large gatehouse which is said to have been the most magnificently furnished in the south-west. It is thought to have been the favourite resting-place of the Black Prince.

During the Prayer Book Rebellion of 1549, Trematon was occupied by Richard Grenville, a loyal supporter of the King, Edward VI. The Cornish rebels, led by Humphrey Arundell, attacked it but were unable to get in. Unfortunately for Grenville, many of his garrison were unwilling to fight and one dark night they climbed out over the walls and ran away. Left with only women, children and a small band of soldiers, Grenville came down to a side gate and tried to talk to Arundell. The rules of battle said that such talks were to be respected by both sides and that no undue advantage was to be taken. However,

Arundell pushed the old man, who was over seventy, to one side and seized the castle. We are told that the inhabitants were not very well treated by the invaders.

With the coming of a peaceful and settled realm, there was no further use for castles. The fine houses built thereafter by the rich and powerful were houses and not fortresses. While they still impressed the people and commanded their respect, they were built with an eye to fine architecture, spacious rooms and large open parks.

St Michael's Mount, the most well-known and famous showplace in Cornwall, has in turn been a monastery, a fortress and a private house and thus is different from the castles just described. Before the first monks arrived there in the eleventh or twelfth centuries, from the similar Abbey of Mont St Michel in France, it had long been a place of religious pilgrimage.

A legend said that St Michael appeared there to some fishermen. Another story said that a giant once lived there. Such an unusual rock, an island at low water and covered with trees, mysterious and haunted, could not fail to be regarded with superstitious awe.

The monks established a chapel on the rock and it became a place for traders. Probably it had been a well-known trading-place for centuries, with a sandy mainland beach and easy access to the tin workings inland. Some say that it was the legendary Ictis, where sailors from the distant Mediterranean came to buy the black tin.

In the early fifteenth century, when there were wars between France and England, the religious links between the Mount and Mont St Michel were broken and it became part of the property of Syon Abbey near London. The stone causeway or break-water was built in 1425 and gave good shelter to the ships, and the town of Marazion grew and flourished. During the next hundred years, it flourished both as a monastery and as a trading centre but its commanding position in the bay meant that it also had possibilities as a fortress.

In 1473, during the Wars of the Roses, when two powerful forces fought a long and desperate civil war in England, the Earl of Oxford, who supported Henry, Earl of Richmond, one of the contenders for the throne, entered the bay by ship and landed his men on the beach. By disguising his men as pilgrims he captured the Mount and turned it into a stronghold. The reigning King, Edward IV, ordered the Sheriff of Cornwall to get it back. The Sheriff was yet another member of the Arundell family, Sir John Arundell, not to be confused with the later man of the same name, the heroic defender of Pendennis Castle in the seventeenth century.

Some years before 1473, someone had put a curse on this Arundell: 'When upon the yellow sand, Thou shalt die by human hand'.

He took it very seriously and went to live at the manor house of Trerice, near Newlyn East, almost as far from the sea as he could get in Cornwall. However, the King's orders were clear and he came to the Mount with his armed men. In the fighting that followed, he was struck down and killed upon the sandy beach. A strange coincidence, or the fulfilment of the prophecy?

The command then fell on Sir John Fortescue, who besieged the mount for twenty-six weeks, by land and sea. The rock was impregnable to direct attack. The only chance of success lay in starving out the defenders or in treachery. Fortescue sent in a stream of secret messages, promising the garrison pardon and reward if they deserted. Realizing that their position was hopeless, they did so, one by one and two by two until only a few were left.

On 15 February, 1473, the Earl of Oxford surrendered and was imprisoned in a castle near Calais for three years before escaping and rejoining his master, Henry, Earl of Richmond. In the last battle of the Wars of the Roses, at Bosworth, he commanded a large part of Henry's army. As you probably know, in that battle the then King, Richard III was killed and Henry became King Henry VII.

The Mount's warlike days were not yet over. In 1497, Perkin Warbeck, who claimed to be the younger of the two Princes in the Tower and took the title of Richard IV, landed at Whitesand Bay by Sennen and collected supporters throughout

St. Michael's Mount

Cornwall. He left his wife at St Michael's Mount and when he arrived at Exeter in September he had an army of many hundreds. His triumph was short-lived and four hundred of his men lay dead on the battlefield and he was a prisoner.

Strangely in such violent days, his life was spared and the king kept him as a scullery boy in the Tower of London for two years. The foolish man then tried to escape, was caught, and this time was executed.

Perkin Warbeck is still remembered in Cornwall. There is an old farmhouse in Bodmin where he is said to have stayed on his journey through Cornwall. He was proclaimed king in the town. In St Ives, Perkin is a common last name although this may be mere coincidence and only the survival of a common enough name in the fifteenth century. After the end of his revolt at Exeter, his wife was captured at the Mount and taken to London where she was honourably treated.

At the dissolution of the monasteries, the Mount passed to the Crown and it became a fortress. Guns were placed there to attack any invading ships and a beacon was built, to act as a lighthouse in peacetime and as part of a warning chain of fires in case of invasion. In 1588, it was lit to warn of the approach of the Armada.

Spanish sea-power recovered quickly after the Armada's disaster and in 1595 the garrison of the Mount were thrown into alarm when a party of Spaniards actually landed in Mount's Bay. It was the nearest approach to an invasion that the country had experienced since 1066.

Early on the misty morning of 23rd July, four Spanish galleys appeared off Mousehole and landed two hundred men who set fire to Mousehole and also Paul, a mile or so inland. Sir Francis Godolphin, a Deputy Lieutenant of Cornwall, thought the long-expected invasion had come and sent a messenger post-haste to Plymouth to warn Drake. He collected a small band of men and marched towards the smoke billowing over Mousehole and Paul. Before he got there, all the Spaniards re-embarked and sailed along the coast to Newlyn where they landed four hundred men, hoping to cut Godolphin off from Penzance. A fierce fight followed and Godolphin was forced to withdraw towards Marazion and the Mount, leaving Newlyn and Penzance to be burned.

By next morning he had gathered many more men and the Spaniards stayed safely at anchor in the bay. The following day, Drake's ships arrived and it seemed that the enemy was trapped. Luck was with them, though. A change of wind enabled them to escape. This was a very frightening event and made everybody in the country realize that invasion was still a real possibility.

When the danger finally passed, Queen Elizabeth sold the rock to the Earl of Salisbury and he later sold it to Sir Frederick Basset, a loyal supporter of Charles I. The Civil War reached it in 1645, by which time the King's cause was lost. Prince Charles, later to become Charles II, stayed there briefly on his way to the Isles of Scilly and exile in France. After his departure, a parliamentary force attacked it by way of a rocky passage, now called Cromwell's Passage. The assault failed but the Governor, Sir Arthur Basset, knew he could not hold out, and surrendered. He and his few remaining defenders were allowed to retire to Scilly. The list of stores and weapons captured includes thirty cannon, eighty barrels of wine, a hundred barrels of gunpowder, five hundred muskets and a hundred pikes.

After the war, in 1647, Parliament chose Colonel John St Aubyn, to be Governor. He was a well-respected figure in Cornwall, having been Sheriff in 1643 and a Member of Parliament for St Ives and Mitchell. The order giving the Mount into his keeping when he went there to live in 1659 is still preserved and reads thus:

To Colonel Robert Bennett,

You are on sight hereof to disband those men under your command in the garrison of St Michael's Mount in the County of Cornwall and to deliver up the possession of the house unto Colonel John St Aubyn, with all the ordnance, arms, ammunition and provisions of war and victuals therein, to be kept by him and possessed for the use of the State, and you are to take a receipt under the hand of the said Col. John St Aubyn of what particulars you shall so have or deliver, and send me a double of them.

Given under my hand, 12th March, 1659,
George Monck, General.

Colonel St Aubyn found it in a poor state, little more than a collection of monastic buildings and a fort. The State had no further use for it and in the same year, the Colonel bought it. Since then, and especially in the eighteenth century, the family has spent much time and money on it, repairing, building and adding, to make the splendid castle home we see today. The pier and harbour was rebuilt in 1727 and the trade in tin and copper from nearby mines was restarted. Today it is owned by the National Trust and lived in by the St Aubyn family, the head of which is Lord St Levan. It is still visited annually by thousands of pilgrims, armed not with Bible and staff but with cameras and plastic macs. The tin trade has gone but an even greater one has arisen, in the car parks and cafés of Marazion.

The other Cornish castles were neither personal homes nor for defence against internal enemies. They were built to guard important harbours against attack by foreign foes.

At Fowey and Polruan, on either side of the harbour mouth, are two ruined forts built in the fifteenth century when lawless men on both sides of the Channel made raids on our coastal towns. The men of Fowey were among them and made frequent pirate attacks on ports in France, earning the nickname of the Fowey Gallants. This name is still borne by the special class of sailing yachts found there. Needless to say, the French retaliated from time to time and in one spirited raid they burned a large part of the town before being driven away. The defence of Fowey was organized by Elizabeth Treffry, whose husband was away at the time. On his return he built or rebuilt the tiny forts and slung a chain between them to prevent the entrance of unauthorised vessels.

The castle at St. Mawes

In the sixteenth century, Henry VIII, faced with enemies in France and Spain, built a chain of coastal defence forts from Cornwall to the Thames. He rebuilt Treffry's forts and added one of his own, St Catherine's Castle. At St Mawes and Pendennis, he built two magnificent castles to protect the River Fal and the port of Penryn. All the latest castle building techniques were used, to produce structures far different from those of the Normans.

Batteries of heavy cannon were housed in strong circular towers and garrisons were kept there all the time. Their living conditions were poor and they literally ate and slept with the guns. They were often not paid for months and more of them died from disease than were killed by any enemy. However, the castles served the purpose the King intended and their threat kept off intruders and invaders. Any ship trying to enter could have been blasted out of the water with ease, while the gunners were well protected from answering fire.

Pendennis Castle

We have read how Pendennis and St Mawes played their part in the king's struggle during the Civil War. Both castles were also used in the two World Wars, 1914–1918 and 1939–1945. Guns were mounted there again to protect the port of Falmouth and Pendennis was used as a naval and military headquarters.

Our Cornish castles now stand in peaceful silence, monuments to man's fear of man and witnesses of our country's history. Whether in ruins or well-preserved, they are now in the care of the Department of the Environment and we hope that they will never again be the scene of any kind of warfare. Many thousands visit them each year but only a few bother to find out anything of their story. Those who do can easily imagine the clatter of hooves on the cobbled courtyards, the busy life that went on there and the watchful faces peering over the old ramparts. Perhaps those with the most vivid imaginations can even see ghosts. Imagination is all that is left to us since there is nobody now living who can tell us the most interesting details.

Few people now remember the days when rich families lived in Cornwall's great manor houses, when horse-drawn carriages trotted up the gravelled carriage-drives and uniformed servants provided every comfort for the ladies and gentlemen. Those days have gone. Not even the richest in the land can now afford to build homes on such a scale and furnish them in such splendour. Even if they did so, the cost of paying servants and keeping the buildings in good repair would be enormous.

Many of the smaller ones have become offices, hotels or flats and most of the larger ones are now owned by the National Trust. The great house of Stowe, home of the Grenvilles, has disappeared altogether. It was a fine place but had a very short life. Built in 1680, it was pulled down in 1720. Trelowarren and Rialton, the ancient homes of the Vyvyans; Godolphin Hall, home of the Godolphin family; Port Eliot, seat of the Earls of St German; and Tregothnan, home of Viscount Falmouth, Caerhays Castle and Trelissick House, are still privately owned and are not yet tourist attractions but the splendid houses of Trerice, built by the great Arundells; Cotehele, built by the Edgcumbes; and Lanhydrock, home of the Robartes family, are all open to the public.

Everyone has a favourite and everyone must make a personal choice but to give one example of what a splendid mansion was like, here is a short description of Lanhydrock, just two miles from Bodmin.

The name is a combination of the Cornish word 'Lan', meaning a monastic property and the name of St Hydrock, an unknown saint who was honoured by the great priory at Bodmin during the Middle Ages. The land was taken by Henry VIII in 1539 when the monasteries were closed and was bought in 1620 by Sir Richard Robartes, a rich merchant of Truro. Between 1630 and 1642 a fine house was built amid rolling parkland and woods. Originally it had four wings surrounding a courtyard but one was removed about 1780.

Lanhydrock House, Bodmin

The family lived here in great style and comfort until one day in 1881 when there was a disastrous fire. In those days there was no national fire service but volunteer fire crews rushed in from Bodmin and Lostwithiel to help the servants and the estate workers. Despite their efforts, all the building, except the north wing, was destroyed. In little more than three years, it was rebuilt in the original style and now appears more or less as it was in the seventeenth century.

It is a comfortable house and it is easy to imagine it being lived in today.

On one side, on the upper floor, is the long gallery which mercifully escaped the fire. It has a ceiling of plasterwork divided into twenty-four main panels, each of which shows a story from the Old Testament. Smaller panels surround it, with carvings of birds and animals. It is thought that the whole ceiling was finished just before the Civil War and it must have taken skilled craftsmen a very long time. The tall windows let in sunlight and air and make it a cheerful room, just the place to relax on a sunny afternoon in summer or in the dark days of winter.

The huge kitchen, rebuilt in 1883, the bakery and the dairy, are fascinating rooms to visit. Here one sees all the tools, pots and pans which were once used to prepare banquets, the cupboards in which the cook, the butler and the housekeeper kept their stores and, best of all, the great open fireplace in which meat was roasted in enormous joints. There is a clever and elaborate arrangement of chains and pulleys in the chimney. By using the rising hot air from the fire, fans turned the wheels and the attached chains turned the meat so that it was properly roasted. Everything is on a grand scale and our kitchens seem very small by comparison. Bread was baked in the ovens every day and in the dairy milk and cream were kept cool and fresh on slate slabs with water running in troughs between them.

Altogether, Landhydrock is a splendid house to visit and the gardens are full of flowers and shrubs. There is a tiny church next to the house, where the family and servants worshipped. On the wall, amid the memorials to the Robartes family, is a piece of writing in Cornish. This is uncommon in Cornish churches, which probably shows how the ancient language was 'old-fashioned' when written wall memorials became usual. This one says, in English translation, 'A straw for tale-bearers'. We wonder why it was chosen and who was the tale-bearer the writer had in mind.

The house and estate were given to the National Trust in 1953 by the Robartes family. Their three centuries of occupation ended in 1969.

79

These were the houses of the rich and famous. How did the ordinary people of Cornwall live? Certainly, they had far humbler dwellings than these. In medieval times, their houses were like those of peasants, fishermen and farmworkers everywhere, small crudely-built cottages with only one or two rooms, simple home-made furniture, no sanitation and open hearths for cooking and warmth. Floors were of beaten earth, or earth mixed with lime-ash, and sometimes covered with rushes or sand from the shore. Walls and roofs were of local materials and in Cornwall there was plenty of granite and slate. Families lived close together, sharing their space with domestic animals, separated only by a partition. Extra room for sleeping was often made by building a platform or loft among the rafters. A ladder gave access and the children could be put there out of the way of the grown-ups around the smoky fire. Such a house, standing alone in the clean fresh air, with a piece of ground for growing vegetables and feeding chickens, goats and perhaps a cow, could be warm and cosy enough but in the towns where they were huddled together with only dark and filthy alleys between them, they were breeding-places for every kind of plague and disease.

In Newlyn, for example, right up to the late nineteenth century, when a drainage system was made, typhoid and cholera were regular visitors, the smell from the houses and the streets was appalling and the water supply from the wells was polluted. With these conditions and the unceasing hard work, men and women were old at forty and many died long before the 'three-score years and ten' which the Bible tells us is man's lifespan.

Other villages and towns were no different. A visitor to Newlyn in the 1880s said that the smell was so bad 'the people here must have wooden noses', and every churchyard in Cornwall has its quota of headstones marking the graves of countless young children, victims of sickness and poverty.

There is said to have been a custom in the mining and country districts that if a house could be built and occupied in one day, it and a small piece of land around it could be claimed as the private property of the builder. It seems incredible that it could be done but the trick was to gather the materials before the set day, to enlist the aid of relations and friends, to start at very first light and work very fast. It was considered 'finished' if, by the end of the day, the roof was on and a fire could be lit. A one-roomed hut, with stones laid dry, that is without cement, and with branches and straw for the roof, might well be built between sunrise and sunset. The owner could then take his time to add the details and improve the work. We do not know how many houses were ever built this way but there are many small barns and cow-houses, intact or ruined, which may once have been the home of a poor family scratching a bare living from the sea or the land.

By the turn of the century, Cornish villages were much as we see them today, small granite or cob cottages with slate or thatched roofs, clustered in terraces or built around cobbled courtyards. The fishing villages had many 'courts', with cottages built over fish and boat cellars at street level and granite steps leading to the houses. St Ives still has many of these old places today,

Whitewashed cottages at Newlyn

The narrow streets and small houses which sprang up in the nineteenth century when Newlyn's fishing was booming

although most of them are now owned by non-Cornish people and used as holiday homes in the summer months. The fish cellars have become garages and they can be sold for high prices far above their original cost. Sadly, many Cornish villages are almost entirely taken over by holiday homes with streets almost deserted between October and May.

At one time, granite houses used to be covered with a thick layer of plaster and then whitewashed. In recent years, it has been the fashion to remove the plaster to reveal the natural beauty of the stone. In the fishing villages much use was made of tarred timber boards and the houses presented a black-and-white front to the world, all tar and whitewash.

As the living conditions of working people improved, so they gathered more possessions around themselves. Pride of place usually went to the kitchen dresser which held cups and saucers and all the other domestic articles. It was the height of luxury to have a parlour or best room, with a plush sofa and chairs and ornaments on the mantelpiece. Such rooms were used only on special occasions, at weddings and funerals, and at Christmas when relatives were entertained, not only to celebrate the occasion but so that the visitors could admire the family possessions.

When a family was especially successful, ownership of a piano was seen as a real mark of fortune. Hundreds of unwilling children were taught to play, whether they had any skill or not. To have a piano, and somebody in the house able to play a tune on it, marked the family as being superior. We may deride this now but these were real family

homes in which every member had pride and where every piece of furniture had been acquired through hard work and sacrifice. By contrast, many houses today seem to be only small hotels, where the members of the family eat and sleep but carry on their social lives somewhere else.

A hundred years ago, many Cornish houses had no proper cooking facilities. Boiling could be done over an open fire in the hearth but baking was difficult as there were few ovens. It was the custom to bake in clay dishes buried in the hot coals, or to use the public bakehouse. Pasties, bread and pies were prepared at home and taken to the bakehouse for cooking. For a very small charge, the baker would put them into his ovens and look after them. Even in the last war, during the 1940s, many of these were still in operation and it was a common sight on Saturday mornings to see the children going through the streets early carrying cloth-covered trays of unbaked goodies and returning at noon with richly-smelling and steaming dinners. How many of them were dropped we shall never know but probably very few as penalties for such disasters were severe. Woe betide anybody who came home minus the pasties.

Although bakehouses were in use up to about forty years ago, their decline began in the later nineteenth century when the Cornish range or 'slab' was invented. This was a magnificent affair. Made of cast-iron it was set in the hearth space and adorned with a great deal of brass. On one side was a covered fire fuelled by coal, on the other was an oven and the top surface, the slab. This was used for boiling water in large black iron kettles. The heat produced on baking days was enormous and in summer the kitchens became unbearable. In winter, no other form of heating was needed and the glow of the fire through the bars was always welcoming and cheerful. They consumed large amounts of coal and made the rooms sooty, particularly in windy weather when gusts down the chimney often filled the room with clouds of smoke. Hundreds of thousands of slabs were made but to find one in good condition today is rare. Most have been thrown out and broken up for scrap.

The oven doors had brass hinges, the fire had a brass ash box, there was a brass fender and overhead there was a brass rail on which to hang cloths. Housewives took great pride in polishing them and Friday was the usual day to do it. The fire was allowed to go out or die down low and the black parts were polished to a high gloss with black lead. The brass was polished and the kettles scoured. It all took hours but the result would have delighted the most severe sergeant-major. With so much soot in the chimney and such roaring fires in the grate, chimney fires were common and many cottages were burned down or badly damaged because of them.

For lighting, candles and paraffin lamps gradually gave way to gas and electric light but there are still many houses in the remoter areas where the former are still used. The older people found it hard to get used to such changes. One old man, in the late 1930s, nearly killed himself and blew up the house because he failed to understand the mysteries of the new gas lamps. On going to bed he turned off the kitchen light and when it went out, turned on the tap again, just to make sure that it was out. He then went to bed and slept peacefully. In the morning, his son came down to find the kitchen full of explosive fumes. As it was still dark he reached for the matches and only remembered in time not to strike one. Had it been the old man who came down first, there would have been a disastrous bang.

Piped water to the houses was something else which came very late to Cornwall. The village pump was the spot where everybody gathered to fill buckets and exchange the latest gossip. Fetching water was generally the children's job, before going to school and again on their return. Mother had to do it during the day. Two buckets were kept in the house, one for drinking and cooking water, the other for 'coddling' water, for washing clothes and floors. Those who lived near a stream were lucky. They could get their 'coddling' water from that and save themselves a walk.

A man who lived in a Cornish village in 1900 tells us of what life was like then. This is how he described a typical week:

Monday was Washday. On Tuesdays, the dried clothes were ironed. On Wednesday, my brother and I took the 'Flasket' (a large wickerwork basket) with the bigger articles to Peggy George, together with two pence. Peggy George kept the mangle, a huge box-like affair weighted with granite boulders which moved on rollers when one turned the handle. It moved wonderfully and we sat on a bench in the kitchen while waiting for a turn. Those who turned the handle themselves paid a penny but we paid two pence because Peggy did it for us. It was quite beyond our power.

On Monday morning, while the washing water was heating, the Sunday clothes were carefully brushed and put away for a week. On Wednesday, all the clean washing was put away into its separate drawers in the chest-of-drawers, the socks darned and the mending done. Thursday was market-day, when the women went to town for butter and eggs and any purchases at the drapers. Friday was the day for cleaning the bedrooms and Saturdays were devoted to general clearing-up and preparation for Sunday. Only the very minimum of work was done on Sundays. All the water needed was fetched on Saturday and a good deal of the preparation of Sunday dinner was also done on that day.

Sunday was a busy day for us children. Sunday School in the morning, then Morning Service, Sunday School again in the afternoon and finally Evening Service. There was nothing optional about it. It was a rule of life and although at times it was very irksome, I find on looking back that it was good discipline and set a standard which we later valued. Sundays gave our mothers something of a rest and they needed it. They worked from morning till night, doing housework, sewing, knitting, cooking and mending. Holidays were unknown and they certainly got none. However long and hard a man worked, a woman had to work a good deal harder.

How times have changed for us all in the last eighty years. With every labour-saving gadget at our command, with water and electric power at our fingertips, with heating systems which regulate themselves automatically, it is hard to realize that this is all 'new' and that there are many still living who lived full lives in what we consider the most primitive way.

Just as the great Cornish homes have become places of business or museums so the ordinary Cornish homes of the last century and the first half of this century have been swept away by the developers or turned into something 'modernized and quaint' by the builder and the estate agent. Those built now are no different from millions of others in the rest of the British Isles. The granite block and the moorland stone have given way to the concrete block and the brick. The Delabole slates have been replaced by the concrete tile. There is now nothing which is distinctly Cornish, either in materials used or in appearance.

If, however, we keep our eyes open and really look at our older houses and cottages, we can still see the real Cornwall and find the things that make a Cornish village so different in appearance from those elsewhere.

Some Things To Do

1 Visit the castles and great houses mentioned.

2 Look for older cottages and houses, cobbled streets, narrow alleys and, in the fishing villages, whitewashed houses and courts.

3 Try to find old photographs of your town and district to see what life used to be like.

Chapter 11

CORNWALL TODAY

The gateway to Cornwall. The modern road bridge and Brunel's 1859 railway bridge at Saltash.

So we come to Cornwall today, having looked at its history from earliest times. We have seen how Cornwall and Cornish people have played their important parts in the general history of Britain and how it has become so much a part of the English scene that it is usually, and quite wrongly, thought of as being English.

The main industry in Cornwall today is tourism. Thousands come here every summer to enjoy the beaches, the cliffs and the sea. The fishermen no longer put out in search of shoals of silvery pilchards as they did in the nineteenth century. They find their shoals, of people, waiting on the quays to be taken for pleasure trips around the bay. Farmers, too, find profit in providing rooms and meals for tourists and thousands of small cottages have become holiday homes for families living far away. Gift shops abound in every town and village and cafes do a roaring trade in a good summer.

All this is good business and we ought to be glad that we live in such an attractive area and that outsiders want to come here for holidays, to open businesses and to retire. Unfortunately, it means that as more non-Cornish folk come in, the Cornish-ness of Cornwall gets less. Most of those who come here to live have no idea of our unique history and no interest in finding out. Too many of our villages are half-empty in the winter, the owners of holiday homes being in Birmingham or Manchester, or some other city in England.

Work outside the tourist industry has always been scarce for the well-educated and well-qualified Cornish person and it is not a comic remark to say that the main export from Cornwall has been Cornishmen. From the days of the great emigration of miners in the nineteenth century to now, there has been a steady procession of young men and women leaving their homeland to seek fortune elsewhere. Few return.

What Cornwall needs is a flourishing home trade of its own, to provide jobs for the young. The resources are here. Minerals abound in the ground, fish are still in the sea and there may be oil under the sea.

Development will cost an enormous amount, far more than is available in Cornwall, so it is likely that any profit will go to non-Cornish pockets.

Farming is important still but farms are small and a long way from the great markets of the cities. It is cheaper to import produce by air from the Continent than to carry it three hundred miles from Cornwall by road or rail. Not many years ago, flower growers in the isles of Scilly and broccoli growers in Cornwall's far west had a ready and profitable market in London, being able to produce daffodils, narcissi, anemones and vegetables long before anybody else had enough sun and warmth. With the growth of air traffic, it is possible to grow these things in Europe in glasshouses and transport them as quickly and as cheaply. Still the flower and early vegetable trade is an important part of Cornwall's economy.

Small factories, employing from twenty to a hundred people, are very common. They are offshoots of larger factories in England, making small parts. They survive because they make specialist equipment which does not require heavy machinery and large supplies of fuel. One large factory in Camborne, Compair, employs several hundreds of skilled men making mining drills and machines for use underground. Its products are sent all over the world. The School of Mines here also trains mining engineers. These two establishments are a direct link with our old mining industry. Shipbuilding, never carried on in a big way, has largely ceased although many yards make yachts and small fishing craft. At Falmouth and Penzance there are ship repair yards, well-known for doing good work in the shortest time.

Bodmin remains the official county town. The chief courts are here but the cathedral and the county government are in Truro. Some say that it is only a matter of time before new courts are built in Truro, and Bodmin loses its status just as Launceston did a century ago.

There is no doubt that historically, geographically and geologically, Cornwall is absolutely different from England. Racially, the true-born Cornishman is as different from an Englishman as is a Welshman, a Scotsman or an Irishman, although we must recognize that through centuries of intermarriage there are not many one hundred per cent Cornish people left. The Celtic characteristics, a love of song and story, an independent spirit, a stubbornness, a certain reserve of manner towards strangers, and a deep feeling of being Cornish, remain. There are still five distinct peoples in the British Isles, English, Welsh, Scottish, Irish–and Cornish. The people of no other county are called by a name ending in 'ish' or 'sh', and this alone marks an important difference.

Nobody disputes that Wales, Scotland and Ireland are not English. Why should Cornwall be considered differently? Its native inhabitants come from the same Celtic stock, it has a language which is basically the same as Welsh, Irish and Gaelic.

It kept much of its native, un-English character until the sixteenth century. Its place-names are largely Celtic, not English. Celtic remains are common and 75 per cent of the church dedications are Celtic.

When the west-bound traveller crosses the Tamar, he recognizes at once that the scenery is changed. The English lushness of pasture and the warmth of its brick, stone and thatched dwellings have given place to bare moorland, few trees, small fields and hedges, scattered villages, grey stone and a strong impression of emptiness in the

Ship repairing at Falmouth today

Truro Cathedral

landscape. In the mining areas, broken mine-stacks point upwards among the gorse and heather, the stone circles and cromlechs stand on the silent uplands and the signposts are full of unusual and hard-to-pronounce names. If he feels that he is in a 'foreign' country, he need not be surprised. He is. This is Cornwall, not England.

Nevertheless, it is classed officially as one of England's forty-six counties and in spite of the efforts of a number of Cornish groups is not yet likely to be recognized as 'independent' in the same way as Wales and Scotland. It is quite possible, though, to keep its Celtic character and spirit alive and it is pleasant to record that there is more enthusiasm for it today than there was forty years ago. Then, there were few people with any knowledge of the language. Books were scarce and it was expected that within a short time all interest would have disappeared. There were many learned books about Cornwall's history but very few for the casually concerned reader.

Strangely in this modern age, all that has changed. There are classes for those wishing to learn Cornish. Annual examinations are held and certificates given for success. Groups meet to talk amongst themselves and there is a playgroup for very small children, where the games and activities are conducted entirely in Cornish. It is called Dalleth = Beginning and it is hoped that the children will grow up to be bi-lingual, as fluent in Cornish as in English. There are now books on

every Cornish subject to suit every taste and interest and the Cornish goods on sale show the great awakening which has occurred.

The most important non-political body of people working for the maintenance of Cornish culture is the Cornish Gorsedd, founded in 1928 to revive and encourage all forms of Cornish language, literature, music, art and science. From being mocked and jeered at in its early days, it has become a much respected organization and it is a great honour for any Cornish man or woman to be invited to become one of its Bards. To be eligible for election one must have worked hard for Cornwall in some way and to have shown a true Celtic spirit. The Gorsedd of Bards meets annually in September, in public on some ancient site, and conduct a simple ceremony in Cornish. It ends with the swearing of loyalty to Cornwall.

No book of this kind can possibly do more than sketch some scenes from Cornish history. It jumps lightly over the centuries, giving no more than a glimpse here and there. If it awakens interest it has done its intended job and if it points the reader in the direction of other, more detailed, books on Cornwall it will have been more than successful. There is much to learn, much to see, much to understand. All of it is fascinating and interesting. This is only the beginning. It is fitting that it shall end with 'Good Luck, Cornwall for ever' in Cornish.

Chons da. Kernow bys vyken.

85

BC

	The Stone Ages
c. 2000	The Megalithic Period
	Cromlechs Stone Circles.

The Stone Ages
c. 2000 The Megalithic Period
Cromlechs Stone Circles.

The Bronze Age
c. 1000 Arrival of the first Celts.

c. 500 **The Iron Age**
The Birth of Christ and the start of our calendar dating.

Map of Cornwall

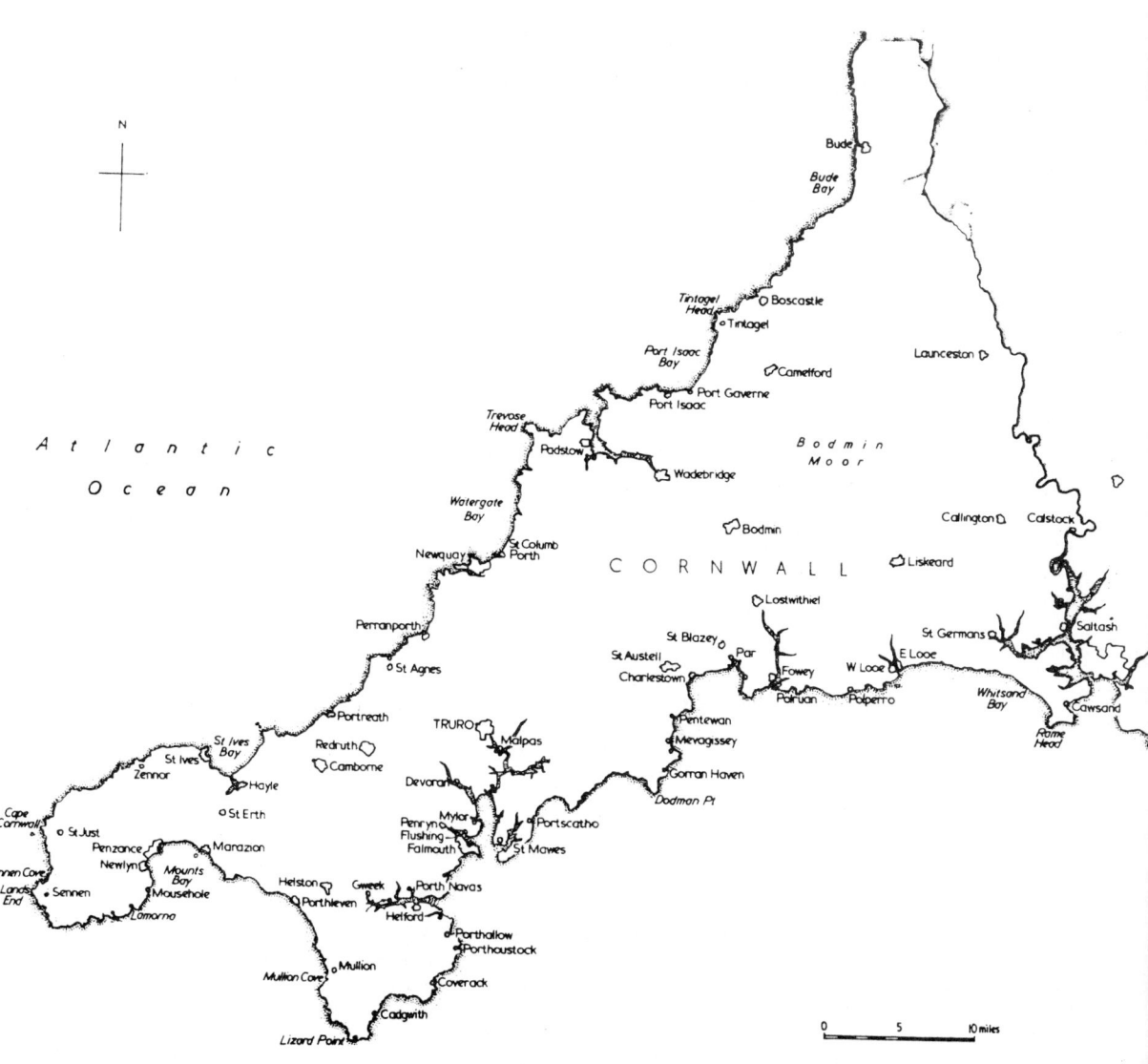

A Date Chart

AD

43–410	Roman occupation of Britain. Trade in Cornish tin.
c. 500–600	English invasion and expansion in Britain.
	Period of Arthur, Doniert and other Celtic kings.
	The age of the saints.
c. 700	English reach the Bristol Channel; Celts of Cornwall cut off from Celts of Wales.
814	English King Egbert conquers Cornwall.
825	Egbert conquers Cornwall for the second time.
838	Battle of Hingston Down. Celts heavily defeated by the English.
c. 928	King Athelstan makes final conquest of the Celts in the west.
1066	Norman Conquest of all Britain.
	Robert of Mortain becomes Earl of Cornwall and builds castle at Launceston.
	Castles at Launceston, Restormel, Trematon and Tintagel built, enlarged or repaired during next five hundred years.
1377	Edward the Black Prince, eldest son of King Edward III becomes the first Duke of Cornwall.
1497	Cornish Rebellion against King Henry VII, led by Thomas Flamank of Bodmin and Michael Joseph of St Keverne. Rebels marched on London. Defeated at Blackheath. Leaders executed. Perkin Warbeck lands at Whitesand Bay, near Land's End and is proclaimed King Richard IV at Bodmin.
	Cornish rebels defeated at Exeter.
1536–1539	Dissolution of the Monasteries.
	Bodmin Priory and other religious houses in Cornwall closed and sold.
1539–1543	Castles at Pendennis, St Mawes and Fowey built.
1545–1549	Loss of the *Mary Rose* and Roger Grenville. Prayer Book Rebellion. Cornish rebels under Humphrey Arundell besiege Exeter and are defeated. Harsh punishments follow in Cornwall.
1577	Cuthbert Mayne executed at Launceston.
1588	Beacon at St Michael's Mount warns of the Spanish Armada.
1591	Death of Richard Grenville in the *Revenge*.
1595	Spanish attack on Penzance, Newlyn, Mousehole and Paul.
1642–1649	Civil War.
1643	Battles of Braddock Down and Stratton. Bevil Grenville killed at Battle of Lansdown.
	King Charles writes letter of thanks to the people of Cornwall.
1646	Siege of Pendennis Castle.
1688	Imprisonment and release of Bishop Trelawny.
1743	John Wesley visits Cornwall for the first time.
1789	Wesley's last visit to Cornwall.
1801	Richard Trevithick's locomotive scales Camborne Hill.
1847	Railway from Plymouth to Falmouth begun.
1852	Railway line from Penzance to Truro completed.
1859	Royal Albert Railway Bridge across Tamar completed.
1850–1865	Period of greatest mining prosperity.
1866	Collapse of copper mining. Mass emigration of Cornish miners.
End of century	Decline of mining and fishing. Rise of china-clay and tourist industries
1919	Levant Mine disaster.
1928	First Cornish Gorsedd at Boscawen-un.
1982	Provision of 'KERNOW' signs on all main roads into Cornwall completed.